LETTERS TO A LOVING GOD

LETTERS TO A
LOVING GOD

A Prayer Journal

ANDREW M. GREELEY

SHEED & WARD
Franklin, Wisconsin
Chicago

As an apostolate of the Priests of the Sacred Heart, a Catholic religious congregation, the mission of Sheed & Ward is to publish books of contemporary impact and enduring merit in Catholic Christian thought and action. The books published, however, reflect the opinions of their authors and are not meant to represent the official position of the Priests of the Sacred Heart.

2002

Sheed & Ward
7373 South Lovers Lane Road
Franklin, Wisconsin 53132
1-800-266-5564

Printed in the United States of America

Cover and interior design by Madonna Gauding

ISBN 1-58051-120-1

INTRODUCTION

The person who appears in this prayer journal is given to complaints, perhaps because he often writes his reflections in the morning when he is not quite awake. He complains about colds, pests, mail, and jet lag; critics who, as he sees it, distort his work; his inability to relax and reflect; the frequent sterility of his spiritual life; distractions when he is working; e-mail; and, oh yes, pests. He does so because he believes that God is the kind of lover with whom you can be candid, especially since God knows what you're thinking about anyway. There's no sense in trying to pose as someone you're not when engaged in intimate conversation with the deity.

Whether readers will like this person is of less importance than whether God does. If there is any theme in these reflections is that God's love is implacable. There's no running from it—and there's no point in trying to run from it. I began to publish these prayer journals in the hope that they would encourage others to keep their own journals. That hope still stands.

May 7, 1999; 10:25 a.m.; Chicago

My Love,

In Milosz's collection this morning, the poet laments her inattention to the "mountain." It is lost to her, sometimes in veils of mist, sometimes to her own inattention. How can one not notice the mountain? Similarly, for me, how can one not notice the city? As I look out my window this morning and see it bathed in the light of the rising sun, glowing and pastel, I realize that it is a kind of man-made mountain, filled with beauty, tragedy, hope, pain, and grace. I must be sensitive to its constant messages and to your presence within it. As I try to rejuvenate my prayer life, the city should be a constant sign of your presence and of your demand for love in response to your love.

I love You.

May 8, 1999; 11:30 a.m.; Chicago

My Love,

In this morning's poem, the author recalls an experience with which I am familiar. Three times he sees women as his train passes them by. He wonders who they are and also whether, if he had them as allies, he could change the world. My experience was the first time I went on a train to the Delta, sixth grade, 1940. As the Illinois Central train moved through the South Side, I saw a family to the left of the train, not on the tracks but perhaps next to the tracks. They were dressed in their Sunday best. One of them was a girl in a white suit about my age; she stood a little apart from the others and I wondered who she was and what her story was. I became aware of her as a person, a thou, for a few moments. I realized that I would never see her again, that our lives had passed each other briefly, and that she would go her own way and I mine, unaffected by that brief night passage of a few seconds which was really a Sunday morning. I still wonder who she was and what happened to her. Weird thoughts for a twelve-year-old boy, huh? Maybe she's dead now, maybe not. Maybe I've met her and never knew it.

I did not fall in love with her in the ordinary sense of the word. I was rather entranced by her as a mystery. Short of paradise, I will never even know her name. She did teach me, however, at least in a simple sort of way, that every human person I encounter is a mystery. But did I reflect in those few moments that You, too, loved her and would take care of her? Or am I reading that back into the world of 1940? Regardless, I know now that You love her and always will and will take care of her and that I can look forward to meeting her again.

I love You.

May 9, 1999; 10:15 p.m.; Grand Beach
My Love,

Mother's Day. Thank You for the grace in my life of my mother who taught me so much. She had a hard life, from beginning to end. I'm sure she's happy with You. Take good care of her for me, I beg You.

This was a glorious day for the celebration of life. The whole world (well, my whole world!) has blossomed in an outburst of spring fertility. Green, green, green—and the blue lake and the blue sky. Nature really does have to struggle to come alive, doesn't it? Eliot was right, though he forgot that May was the cruelest month of the year in midwest America—as was Fr. Hopkins. Is the struggle of nature to surmount death each year part of your ongoing struggle with the forces of disorder and chaos? At any rate, it is a sacrament of that struggle. I renew my faith today in the sacramental fertility of spring. I love it . . .

And I love You.

May 10, 1999; 10:35 a.m.; Grand Beach
My Love,

It is so lovely up here. I relax almost upon arrival. It is a very good feeling. I find myself thinking this morning that I am not entitled to such beauty and peace, especially since I have yet to learn how to give myself over to it. Yet, I am grateful for the pure gift that it is. I do not have, in the ordinary nature of things, all that many Grand Beach summers left. Help me to revel in this one and those which will come after it.

Is heaven like Grand Beach? Perhaps I should put it this way. Grand Beach, on a lovely May Monday like this one, gives a hint of heaven. So that makes me very happy.

I love You.

May 11, 1999; 9:55 a.m.; Chicago
My Love,

The flowering trees are so gorgeous this time of the year. More than anything else they represent the explosion of spring. Yet, the blossoms fade so quickly. We enjoy them for a few days or a week—and then they're gone. I have often thought this spring that the blossoms on the trees are like human life: sweet, fragile, delicate, and short-lived. We are blown away like the fading spring blossoms after a brief flirtation with existence. No getting away from it.

However, while we have life and with full knowledge of its fragility, we must live, no matter how weary or tired we become. I thank You for my life. Help me to devote whatever is left to a more generous response to your love.

I love You.

May 12, 1999; 9:15 a.m.; Chicago
My Love,

A kind of sleepy morning after a difficult day yesterday. Time keeps slipping away.

The poem this morning tells of a train ride through Norwegian mountains. The poet feels sorry for the people who live such narrow lives in the tiny villages he passes through. But perhaps they are happier than he is. As I, of all people, ought to know, cosmopolitans are no less narrow, no less rigid, no less insensitive than locals. At least the locals are not snobs!

His reaction was nothing like mine to the girl we passed so long ago on the IC tracks. I saw a "thou." He saw only inferior people he wanted to liberate. Different context, indeed. I must try to see people without prejudgment. And to smile. Oh, I must smile whenever I can. Help me to smile to show that You love everyone. Not an oily snickering smile, but a real, happy smile.

I love You.

May 13, 1999; 10:39 a.m.; Chicago
My Love,

I gave a lecture about doctors and religion at the university hospital yesterday. It went well. I found the hospital, like all hospitals, to be a depressing place, even when they are new and elegant. What is depressing, of course, is our own frailty and mortality. The only response I can think of to death just now is to say that we should laugh at it and trust in You. Somehow this morning that doesn't seem so consoling—but it's a gray grim morning.

I love You anyway.

May 14, 1999; 9:20 a.m.; Chicago
My Love,

I am losing my temper often these days, which probably isn't a good thing, is it? Part of it is the pressure of getting ready for the trip to Europe. However, there is also the fact that I am being hounded by the idiots. I was so angry at the editor of a national magazine yesterday that I woke up angry this morning. I am too old for such rages, however justified they may be. Right?

So when he calls back, I must strive to be calm, not for him—because he's rude and arrogant and insufferable—but for myself. None of the problems is worth my losing my cool over. I'm sorry. I'll try not to do it again.

I love You.

May 17, 1999; 9:40 a.m.; Over the North Atlantic on the way to London and Rome
My Love,

Off on another foolish trip—two weeks this time to London and Rome and Köln. We've started off badly: an hour-and-a-half delay on the runway in Chicago because of the rain, which means we'll probably miss our connection at Heathrow and, even if we make the connection by the skin of our teeth, we'll leave our baggage behind. Mistake not to use carry-on luggage all the time.

Anyway, I am resolved to be patient, which I was usually in Madrid—though not always. So far I have been patient, helped by a nap before I left for the airport . But I am wary of the days ahead. It's been a long, long time, since I've been abroad this long a time.

In the poems I read the day before yesterday about travel, there was a common theme, according to Milosz: the search for community by the poets with those they encountered on their travels. I suppose that's what I was looking for when I discovered the girl on the side of the railroad track so long ago: a sense of common humanity. Let me try to remember that insight for all the people I will meet on this trip. They are all your children, and I must respect and be patient with them. Take care of me, I beg you, on this trip.

I love You.

May 21, 1999; Rome
My Love,

While I find St. Peter's and the Vatican and the Curia all excessive, the faith of the people who come here to pray is often impressive—and my cynicism depressing. I'm sorry. I'm glad, however, of the opportunity to come here and take on my own attempts at balancing the complexities. Thank You. Take good care of me, please.

I love You.

May 26, 1999; Köln
My Love,

Five o'clock. Couldn't sleep for the first time on this venture. Also very fatigued. I'll be balancing a lot these next few days. Can't get the e-mail working, either. Help me to hold together. More reflections when I get home.

I love You.

May 27, 1999; Köln
My Love,

Both papers went well. Tomorrow is a day off. The swimming pool is great. The e-mail is working again. For all of which, many thanks.

I love You.

May 28, 1999; Köln
My Love,

I spent most of the day touring Romanesque churches here in Köln. Very lovely. What enormous energy and dedication went into rebuilding them after the war. As I say, in another thousand years few people will notice that they are restorations. How very Catholic. So many things to reflect on when I get home.

I love You.

May 31, 1999; Frankfurt
My Love,

Memorial Day. Prayers for all those who died in wars and for those who are fighting them today.

Home today from a hectic but enjoyable trip. Now there remains only the journey to Tampa on Wednesday and Thursday—and then Grand Beach. Thank You for the excitement of the trip and for taking care of me during it.

I love You.

June 2, 1999; On the way to Tampa
My Love,

June already! Not fair! I'm on my way to give the academic address for Bob Burns's promotion to the rank of Master of Sacred Theology by the Dominican Order, a richly deserved honor. I'm exhausted, half sick, disoriented, spiritually numb. In addition, on return after two weeks away, I was greeted with manuscripts for four books and foolish questions from editors or copy editors. So tired.

Anyway, at Grand Beach, beginning tomorrow, I will begin to rehabilitate myself.

I love You.

June 4, 1999; 10:25 a.m.; Grand Beach
My Love,

Here at last! For which, thank You very much. I'm so tired. Busy unpacking and organizing. Help me to settle in and settle down.

The current issue of *Poetry* has several poems that are excellent reflection material. So I turn to them as I try to put back in place my emotional, spiritual, and physical health. The one today is about a man at the side of a pool closing his eyes to obscure the beautiful setting so he can imagine other beautiful settings he will never see and lament that loss. Kind of convoluted, but I see his point: movements of wanters and leavers, as he said, which will never again occur. I could say that the picture of the lake and the beach I barely noticed today is something that will never recur again. I have lost it.

There will be other pictures tomorrow and, of course, my *Songs of a Lunatic* this summer. Moreover, one cannot grasp every single moment and one would go crazy if one tried. Yet, one can enjoy, revel in, and even become overwhelmed by occasional moments. I must give myself over to that this summer—more often than I have in the past. In fact, however, the poet is right: it is a shame that we cannot spend all our time reveling in the beauties with which You bombard our lives.

I love You.

June 5, 1999; 9:10 a.m.; Grand Beach
My Love,

I hear the sound of the wave runners, see a sailboat on the lake, feel the flies biting at my legs, see the kids jumping into the frigid lake, absorb the heat and the humidity. A summer day before its time. Glorious! Thank You. The poet I read today talks about her husband's seventy-fifth birthday as he works on a summer garden. She concludes, "Summer afternoon is all there is / and night will never fall."

She's right, of course. Except night will fall. But it will never put out a summer afternoon. This I absolutely believe.

I love You.

June 6, 1999; 8:15 a.m.; Grand Beach
My Love,

I'm not sleepy any more, for which, many thanks, but I still lack energy. I look at the pile of papers I must bring to the recycle bin and then move outside and then leave them there. I look at the clock, which must be rewound, and not touch it. Exhaustion. But I make progress of a sort.

The poem today talks not about summer days but summer nights and kids chasing fireflies (which they release), then the poet concludes, "another evening's/praise for this uncertain, only life." Why, when they can write such lines, do contemporary poets write such opaque rubbish?

Anyway, "uncertain, only life." How wonderful! I believe in more life and life superabundant, but it is the only life we know. Summer evenings—regardless of the heat, like we have now, and the bugs—are wonderful sacraments, hints of transcendent beauty and goodness, hints of You. The sea birds created a big racket this morning. I hadn't noticed them yet. More sacraments, sacraments all around us.

I love You.

June 7, 1999; 8:20 a.m.; Grand Beach
My Love,

The poet this morning is John Updike, who tells us that he values more freeing a finch which was trapped in his house than the words he as written. However, he does not stop writing the words. Nor should he. How does one sort out the various activities in one's life and find meaning and purpose in them? I confess I don't know. In the last couple of days, as I try to put myself back together again, I have been reflecting on what I have made of my life. Especially as I think about what I will say at the American Sociological Association's (ASA) "appreciation" of my work, I realize how little I have accomplished and how quickly I will be forgotten. Who has a right not to be forgotten? We pass and will be forgotten with the rest!

So much conflict, much of it over what I considered principle, integrity, honesty, some of that marred by anger (as I am still angry at the AARP). So little peace and tranquility. So much defensiveness (and so much attacking by others). It all seems silly, pointless, a waste of time. Just as Aquinas said. I have worked terribly hard and still do, but for what purpose? So it is that I always think during my acclimation to summer here at Grand Beach. These thoughts usually do not last. Perhaps they should.

I love You.

June 8, 1999; 8:40 a.m.; Grand Beach
My Love,

Today's poem is about a priest (or a cleric, but probably a priest) out in the prairies, and all he thinks about as he prepares for services—images from around the world and from his parish. He realizes that he is a bit of a rock, a spear of grass, a brief disturbance on the prairie. Then he puts on his collar, adjusts it carefully, and "and makes his way past the lilacs towards the church."

Not all priests are that reflective. Some of us are. Whether we are or not, we must make our way past the lilacs towards the church. My way is a little different—no a lot different. I am dissatisfied with it now. But then, aren't we all dissatisfied with our lives. Maybe I think too much. Or imagine too much. Or lament lost opportunities too much. Help me.

I love You.

June 9, 1999; 8:10 a.m.; Grand Beach
My Love,

The poem this morning is about a novelist who claims to try to sum up the lives of his characters in a single sentence. Interesting idea. How would I sum up my life in a single sentence (not to say that of my characters who will have to wait till I get back to them!)?

How about: "He was afraid to stop running for fear he'd never be able to start again!" Ouch! Where did that sentence come from? Or: "He could never understand why people who didn't know him hated him." Or: "He never knew how to draw the line on his area of responsibility." I'm not sure I like this game! No, I don't like the game at all.

But I do love You.

June 10, 1999; 8:45 a.m.; Grand Beach

My Love,

Who are You, anyway? And what do You want of me? I found myself wondering that this morning. Who You are is, of course, unanswerable, but I think I have learned more about that through the years. What You want of me, however, has become progressively less clear. I just don't know—not at all, at all. My life is running out and I wonder, not whether I should have done it all differently (not exactly) or even what I would do if I could do it all over again (bootless), but how I might try to do what remains, even at the cost of breaking out of the pattern in which I now live.

I discovered this morning that I hadn't taken my thyroid medicine for four days. No wonder I'm spaced out.

Thank You that the Kosovo war is over.

I love You.

June 14, 1999; 9:05 a.m.; Grand Beach

My Love,

What, indeed, do you want of me? What might I do differently? Perhaps you want me to stop asking that question and simply relax and enjoy the summer. I shall try to do that. I could say that I have earned the right to relax and refresh and write poetry. But that right is a given, not earned. So I had better exercise it, had I not?

I love You.

June 16, 1999; 11:55 a.m.; Grand Beach

My Love,

Why do I have these rectory dreams? I seem to have dreams about every rectory I've ever lived in—even the St. Angela rectory in which I never lived. I know—or think I know—the triggers, but the substance of the dream, which is always the same . . . ? I am newly assigned to the parish and encounter priests who are skeptical but not hostile. Something like the trauma of my move from Christ the King (CK) to St. Thomas. Probably at some deep level it is my ambivalence about my *de facto* isolation from the archdiocese, one which I hope will go away but which I know will not. Anyway, it is good that I am what I am and where I am. Anything that changes the situation, however moderately, is also good, but I must be cautious and skeptical about it. I am who and what and where You want me to be, however imperfectly I live up to what You would like me to be. Help me to get better at it.

I love You.

June 17, 1999; 8:10 a.m.; Grand Beach
My Love,

For some reason I feel very fragile this morning. No, I know the reason—or at least part of the reason. There are some repairs and modifications needed in the house. I wonder whether I'll be around long enough to see them. Silly fear. One must do what must be done. Regardless. Still . . .

Also, I tried to do a little writing yesterday and find that I simply am not motivated to do it. I need more rest and more rest it will be. But when before have I not wanted to write? Yet, it is such a beautiful day: blue sky, cotton-candy clouds, surf on the beach, germaniums blooming at pool side. Why don't I rejoice in what is instead of worrying about what should be? More rest needed? So what!

I love You.

June 19, 1999; 8:50 a.m.; Grand Beach
My Love,

In Tom Groome's book there is a chapter on "dangerous moments" in one's family history. What was the most "dangerous moment" that I can remember? I'm sure it was the time when my mother told me that my father could have made a million-dollar profit if he had been willing to pay a million-dollar bribe to Mayor Anton Cermak. Looking back on the history of that time, most men would have considered it nothing more than the cost of doing business. Dad turned him down flat and thus kept us respectably poor. I don't quite have that stubborn integrity, but I have enough of it to refuse to be corrupted by either the Church or the academy. Nor am I likely to do so now. I'll cheerfully accept whatever validation comes my way, but no compromise.

Some of this is your work, too. You never really put me in a situation in which I could easily sell out. Both You and my father never gave me much choice, for which, many thanks. Yet, I must not sit in judgment on those who have.

I love You.

June 20, 1999; 8:40 a.m.; Grand Beach
My Love,

I went waterskiing for the first time this summer. Got up promptly and felt great. Admittedly, I came home and slept for two hours, but I didn't have to take another nap this afternoon as I did last year. I had forgotten how much skiing improves my sense of well-being. It is absurd that someone my age still plays at the game, but You have given me the health and the physical condition that makes it possible—for which I am very, very grateful. I promise that I will not overdo it—or take long naps if I have!

On the beach today I remarked at how little kids are getting. I marveled at them chasing after one another on the beach and playing with their fathers on Father's Day. So much beauty in the world. Kids get smaller every year!

I'm reading a Vatican Observatory book on science and religion, which purports to show how You work in the world in and through the processes of the natural law. It's very impressive. You are really very clever. I like one point: What kind of God is it whose mind can be penetrated by human sciences? One with remarkable ingenuity and humor of a sort, especially to come up with quantum mechanics. Your humor stands to be tested by how good You are at wiping away the tears. I mean, I believe You can, but we humans want to see it. Eventually.

Thank you for the peace in Kosovo. Please, please let there be peace in Northern Ireland.

I love You.

June 22, 1999; 8:30 a.m.; Grand Beach
My Love,

I missed a reflection yesterday on Midsummer's Day, St. John's night, whatever one calls it, because I went to Chicago for a funeral. (Take care, please, of Dan Goggin and his family.) The longest day of the year, still light when I got back here at 9:00. Now the days get shorter, which, as You know, makes me unhappy. Anyway, now that it's really summertime, thank You once again for summer.

I have been reading an interesting book about evolution and theology, which addresses itself to how there's room left for You in an evolutionary universe. Some of the authors say that You created it, set the rules, and sustain it in being. Others say that You wheel and deal in the indeterminism of the quantum world, especially by presiding over the genetic mutations—an especially objective intervention, whatever that means. If the latter be true, I think that's pretty clever and also pretty sneaky.

I believe that all systems are basically open and that perhaps the theologians have worried too much about Darwinism. I believe also in a special subjective intervention in which You are involved all the time, without violating the laws of nature which You established. How You do that I do not know. That You do it, I don't doubt. Whether the scientists and the theologians will figure it out, I don't know. I hope they do, however, because it would make things easier, pastorally, for us to explain how You work. There is something just a little absurd about trying to figure that out, isn't there? A God that could be figured out wouldn't be God. But perhaps we can figure out a little more.

My own guess is that You work, somehow or other, in the act of sustaining everything in being.

Anyway, I know You are around—and I love You.

June 23, 1999; 8:40 a.m.; Grand Beach
My Love,

I finished the book on biology and religion. My conclusions:

1) Many of the Darwinists like Dawkins are metaphysical imbeciles.
2) Many of the theological responses to them are clever, necessary, and dull.
3) The debate does not advance my knowledge about You, or about the problem of evil, at least not very much.

However, those things being said, I did learn a lot from the essay by my old friend John Haught about You as vulnerable God. Ought not it be clear to us that the Incarnation revealed that You suffer with us? You have emptied yourself for us. How this works I don't understand, but that it happens, I do believe. Does it go on in the indeterminacy of the quantum world or in your sustaining the whole world in existence? I do not know, but I do know that the very hairs of my head are numbered and that not a sparrow falls from the sky without your involvement. One must cling to those gospel truths regardless.

A lot of anger in me lately. I don't know why. Haven't rested enough yet.

I love You.

June 28, 1999; 8:05 a.m.; Grand Beach
My Love,

Waterskiing on Lake Michigan yesterday. Glorious experience!

I'm rushing to get all my work done by July 1. How often have I been down this path before! Sorry!

I love You.

June 30, 1999; 8:15 a.m.; Grand Beach
My Love,

Two very stressful days as I tried to cope with another person's cynicism and disillusion. So very sad. I pray that all will be well. These may be good times for me, but they are bad times for the Church. When will things change? Will they in my lifetime?

I doubt it. I do trust, however, that You know what You are doing.

I love You.

July 6, 1999; 8:49 a.m.; Grand Beach

My Love,

I got stressed out with all the guests and activities over the holiday. Tired. Lost my temper. Sorry. At least the heat wave is broken. I slept well last night, and I feel much better. For all of which, many thanks. I'm sorry that I became catatonic. There was too much going on. Now I hope I can settle down at least for some days of what I wanted summer to be.

I was inexcusably angry during the weekend. No, I take that back. I had some excuse for my anger, but it was still not right or proper and I'm sorry.

I'm sure that thoughts of mortality plague me. Also, the sense that my summer is being taken away by people. However, too much heat and not enough sleep are surely part of the problem. Actually, I was terrible! Really! I don't think people noticed except that I was tired because I didn't sleep.

The waterskiing was pretty good, however.

Anyway, it's good to be back on track. Thank you for all the graces of the weekend.

I love You.

July 7, 1999; 8:38 a.m.; Grand Beach

My Love,

I'm back to my spiritual reading—at last! This morning I read about the mysterious trial of faith that St. Thérèse experienced during the last months of her life, something that echoed John of the Cross's Dark Night. I do not pretend to understand these phenomena. But I do know that many of us are endlessly plagued by doubts, and that these doubts can be especially strong as death draws near. I have learned the hard way that doubts and faith coexist. I find myself on occasion arguing that however weak the rational arguments may seem, the poetic arguments are unanswerable—and I fall back on them as superior knowledge, at least in time of crisis. How will I react at the time of my death? With your help I will believe in the light, no matter how great the darkness. Please strengthen my faith, especially when I am tired or worn out.

I love You.

July 8, 1999; 8:13 a.m.; Grand Beach

My Love,

The only way to think constructively about death is to surrender to it. A workman said this morning, apropos the new stairs I had put in on the way down to the beach (much safer for both kids and adults), that it would last a long time. I thought to myself that it would last a lot longer than I would. I am fixing up a lot of things in the house, most of which are long overdue because I finally have found a contractor I can trust. I will, in the ordinary course of events, enjoy these improvements for a lot less time than I put up with the old aggravations. The house will outlast me.

Finally, the response to that is, so what? One is given a life to live and one lives as best one can. When it comes to an end, there will be something much better waiting. One must accept the incompleteness of life, the inevitability of death, and the promise—your promise—of what is to come. One must neither deny death nor be preoccupied by it. I don't think I do either. However, it does bother me. The thought of it sneaks up when I'm not prepared for it, intrudes in my life, and takes away some of the joy of life. That must be resisted and, with your help, I will resist it.

I love You.

July 13, 1999; 8:20 a.m.; Grand Beach
My Love,

A lot about aging and death in the last few days, especially at Bob Podesta's funeral. For a few moments, it was CK forty-five years ago, and we were all young again. Which I believe is what it will eventually be like—and so I said in my homily.

As for that which intervenes between now and then, the only thing to do is to surrender and accept whatever death, whenever and however. Acknowledging that truth, however, does not eliminate the melancholy.

Strengthen my faith and courage, I beg you.

And help me to love You more and more.

July 14, 1999; 7:55 a.m.; Grand Beach
My Love,

Yesterday I read a poem in *Poetry* called "The Republic of Longing." It is a strange poem in which the author describes vividly an imaginary country to which he longs to return. It is a charming, enticing, romantic place. Then he hears the voice inside him warning him that he must leave, go home at once, and never return. He must get out while he still can. I interpret the poem as meaning that we must escape from fantasy before we confuse it with reality—obviously a prosaic interpretation of beautiful imagery.

I ask myself about my own fantasies, harmlessly acted out in my stories, but still permeating my life. I suppose I have come to terms with the fact that I can't have my cake and eat it too—I can't be the critic, the square peg, and still expect to be accepted. I can't be all the things I am and still be a man approved in my city, my university, my Church. How could I have ever thought I might be! What is remarkable is that I am as accepted as I am. Yet, I continue to be involved in behind-the-scenes machinations to influence what happens in these institutions. Nothing wrong with that, but I must not deceive myself with the fantasy that what I do matters.

I have gone north which precludes going south. Still, at some level, it doesn't seem fair.

Anyway, it doesn't really matter any more.

I love You and You love me, which is what really counts.

July 18, 1999; 8:23 a.m.; Grand Beach

My Love,

Summer is now more than half over. Ugh! I protest! But just like life, and all good things, we wait for them, and they come and then slip through your fingers. Well, thank You, anyway, for life and summer—and all good things.

Back today from the Goggin wedding in Chicago, a day of triumph for that resourceful and deeply religious family. Thank You for bringing them into my life and for permitting me to serve them through the years.

Yesterday was a strange day. There was an attack on my fiction ("potboilers") in the AP religion column and a lunch with John Piderit, who understands and loves the stories. How can novels stir up such different reactions? Beats me. And bothers me, too. However, people do like them and that's what counts. I often wonder how much more good they would do if it were not for the prejudice against them? But that's your problem, not mine.

I love You.

July 19, 1999; 8:11 a.m.; Grand Beach

My Love,

Marie Ponsot in the poem I read this morning tells the story of an old wine lord who made his best wine ever out of rotten grapes. Ponsot concludes "age is not/all dry rot/it's never too late/sweet is your real estate."

It's never too late. Of course it is never too late. Sometimes I find myself thinking that there's no point of trying anything more because I won't live to finish it or see it or take advantage of it. Yet, in fact, it is altogether possible that my best work, my most important work, remains to be done. That would be true even if I knew certainly when I will die. It's never too late.

Have You not given me enough proof in my life of that truth? Old age is not all dry rot.

I love You.

July 21, 1999; 8:45 a.m.; Grand Beach

My Love,

Bad night. Emergency call in the middle of night. Prayers for all concerned. Sorry for being upset (internally) by the disturbance. House swarming with people today: cleaners, repairers, builders. My fault for scheduling too much. Next three days should be good.

Great Ponsot poem this morning, comparing a polychrome statue of the

Madonna with a young woman walking out of Notre Dame (cathedral, as if You didn't know). Both signs of grace in the world. Grace is everywhere!

I love You.

July 22, 1999; 9:15 a.m.; Grand Beach
My Love,

The poem this morning is about swimming in the sea—odd, since shortly I'll be swimming in the lake as I ski on Michigan, which isn't really a lake but a fresh water sea.

How little I appreciate either the lake or swimming. How little I appreciate all the good things with which You have overwhelmed me. I'm sorry. This morning I will try to revel in the lake.

I love You.

July 24, 1999; 8:55 a.m. Grand Beach
My Love,

You owe me a favor! I'm kidding of course. I owe *You* favors for all the gifts You have given me. I was delighted that I had a chance to say a few things about You on TV yesterday in the midst of the terrible stuff about poor John Kennedy's death—that You love us like a mother loves her child, that You will not permit us to taste death. It wasn't much, I admit, but I didn't have much time. Grant peace to him and his wife and sister-in-law and his family. Protect us all from the media vultures.

Do I believe what I said? Surely I do, even if I don't understand how You work and always have questions on the level of head, even if I am overwhelmed by the poetry. Fog hoods me, Ponsot writes this morning, but the hood of fog is sun!

Yes, indeed, and the hood of sun is You.

Incidentally, I don't blame You for the weather, though I know You are involved in it some way or the other. But this constant heat is terrible.

Despite all the mystery, I know that You are doomed to love us—me.

So I try to love You in return.

July 25, 1999; 7:55 a.m.; Grand Beach
My Love,

I am sad today for reasons that You understand and which I don't need to put on disk. The sadness results from tragedies I observe and do not understand. How can these awful life-wasting situations occur? How can such monumental self-deception and self-destruction take place? In both cases, there seems to be nothing I can do. One was lost long, long ago. The other? There is nothing I can do, it seems, though the loss is not yet certain. I wrack my brains. Why should I succeed when others closer and better qualified have failed? I tried once before in vain, with a disastrous explosion. Try again without much hope of success—and I could rupture the relationship completely.

I don't know what to do. I must talk and think and pray for your illumination. Perhaps it must be left to time to do its healing. But it hasn't so far.

And then I wonder about myself. Do I have similar needs to control everything? Am I engaged in self-deception and self-destruction? I don't think so, but what do I know! Bad business. For the present, I do nothing. Help me.

I love You.

July 26, 1999; 8:50 a.m.; Grand Beach

My Love,

Ponsot's poems this gloomy, hot, and humid Monday morning fit my gloomy mood. Why gloomy? I don't know! Summer slipping away, things breaking, general weariness—the problem mentioned yesterday. Dread of the ASA festivities. All silly and foolish. My happiness ought not to be invested in dubious ventures and their dubious success.

Also, a sense of abandonment and failure, those perennial temptations. Or maybe not. How can I read the e-mail about my novels and think I'm a failure. Yet, life slips through my fingers and gets lost in silly things— like calling to repair a printer. What nonsense!

Monday morning is never a good day anyway. I should be enjoying myself and I am not. I will try my best to cheer up.

I love You.

July 29, 1999; 10:29 a.m.; Grand Beach

My Love,

I am impressed again this morning with the vanity of all human activities. Vanity of vanities, chasing after the wind, as Qoheleth says. Maybe the reason is that I slept poorly last night or maybe the interminable heat spell. However, as I view my life and all my efforts, I realize how trivial they are and how trivial I am. I have worked very hard for all my years in the priesthood and . . . and what? And I have nothing to show for it? That's ridiculous. Rather, it's the sense that my work doesn't make much difference and will be easily and quickly forgotten.

Ponsot this morning describes figures in the *Book of Kells* looking fearful (awed, I think she means) as they learn the meaning of shooting stars. Wow! What is the meaning of shooting stars? After all the books about science and religion I have read, I don't know. Yet, they must have meaning. What meaning?

The incomprehensibility of everything and my triviality in the midst of everything are (perhaps) the reason I feel this morning that all is vanity. I even wonder how You can find time to care about me—and even why You should.

I love You.

July 30, 1999; 10:43 a.m.; Grand Beach
My Love,

Much better today. The problems don't go away. How can they? After all, they are the problems of mortality. However, a pretty good sleep, wonderful waterskiing on the lake—and somehow life looks better, despite the heat, which is the worst I can remember (and the lake is 79 which is virtually unthinkable). But what kind of faith is it that is based on sleep and waterskiing?

The poet this morning says that all stories are about leaving home at dawn and coming back at dusk. This is certainly true in my novels, though I'm not always conscious of it (sometimes I am). It is also true in life. We go forth, we travel, then we come home—at the end of the day or the month or the year or life.

What a puzzle life is. What a puzzle we are. What a puzzle You are. The most complicated puzzle of all.

But still I love You.

August 2, 1999; 10:38 a.m.; Grand Beach
My Love,

The weather broke yesterday—hottest July on record!—and I turned off the a/c, opened all the windows in the house, and let the breezes and the fresh air pour in. Wonderful! Then I went skiing and came back with the marvelous blend of exhilaration and relaxation, which is usually the consequence of skiing (followed often, though not yesterday, by sleepiness). The world suddenly seemed a very good place, which, of course it is. Thank You much.

Ponsot this morning says she looks at the world and sees not cosmos but cosmogenesis. She suggests that she thus rejects Aristotle, but not really. The cosmos is still in the making, You are still expressing and revealing yourself in it—in the flowers and the lake and the breezes, and in my well-being. I have a hard time believing that each one of us is part of that self-revelation, but I do believe it just the same. Help me to believe it more, so I can be more confident in your goodness.

I love You.

August 3, 1999; 9:30 a.m.; Grand Beach
My Love,

This morning the poet says that you cannot leap from the true to the beautiful because it is irresponsible and unpopular. However, she seems ready to proceed to the argument that you can leap from the beautiful to the true, from a lovely statue to the truth that we are always in the hand of love.

I believe that we are, indeed, always in the hand of love. Poetically, there can be no doubt about that. On more prosaic grounds, the question is much more confused, but the answer ultimately must be the same.

So, in return, I try my best to love You.

August 4, 1999; 9:32 a.m.; Grand Beach

My Love,

This morning the poet has some odd lines: "fear of the beautiful roots under the roots of fear." Why is the beautiful fearful? Perhaps because it is overwhelming, perhaps because it promises so much. Perhaps because we are afraid of being deceived—Rudolph Otto's *tremens* and *fascinans!*

Surely the Church has been ambivalent about the beautiful, especially the beauty of the human body. Yet, in its best moments, it knows that beauty is the most powerful hint of You. If there is beauty, then there is Beauty—and Beauty perhaps ought to be feared but after fear, as in the poem, it should be loved.

I love You.

August 5, 1999; 9:27 a.m.; Grand Beach

My Love,

Into Chicago today for four nights, right in the middle of the best time of the summer!

No choice. Interesting days and interesting challenges, as You well know. Help to be patient and keep everything under control. And also to be charming.

I love You.

August 7, 1999; 10:05 a.m.; Chicago

My Love,

Well today is officially "Andrew Greeley Day" in Chicago. That and a dollar and a half will get one a ride on Mayor Rich's subway. Moreover, the symposium in appreciation of my work will not substantially alter my image as either a sociologist or a priest. Those who like me will be pleased; those who don't will hardly notice. It is nice that the cardinal is coming to the symposium. Indeed, the whole thing is nice—and for that I'm grateful. But hardly overwhelmed. Still, I must thank You for the graces with which You have inundated me during my life. You have been very generous. Help me to be generous in return.

I love You.

August 8, 1999; 8:15 a.m.; Chicago

My Love,

Sunday night. The sun has just set. The last night of these four nights in Chicago. Back to Grand Beach tomorrow—where I belong this time of the year.

The ASA session yesterday was very successful—a four-part exposition of my work as a sociologist, which presented as an adequate sketch of this dimension of my life as I could possibly have expected and made me feel that I was more of a success than I had ever thought possible. The cardinal came to the session and stayed afterwards at supper until 8:00. He genuinely admires me and my work, which astonishes me.

This weekend has been a great grace for me, for which I am very, very grateful. I am sorry that I didn't realize how much I have accomplished, perhaps because much of it was done in times of stress and distraction. I tried to persuade myself that the weekend was not important—when it really was very, very important Thank You for everything.

I love You.

August 11, 1999; 11:08 a.m.; Grand Beach

My Love,

Back at the lake. Two lovely days. Skiing both days. Feel wonderful. Thank You. I experienced a bit of a letdown after the weekend. No question that it was a good event, which confirmed the value of a lot of what I have done as a sociologist. Not everyone would agree—but enough people do so that I can feel content with my work. Now back to the poetry!

I love You.

August 13, 1999; 8:13 a.m. Grand Beach

My Love,

Mike Rochford is dead. And as is usually the case, I'm tied up here and can't make it to the funeral. Grant him peace and joy and happiness.

Far be it for me to criticize your plans . . . *but* he was such a gifted person with so much promise, much of which was never realized because of bad health and perhaps other factors. So many others too, especially priests, of which I can think on this gloomy subject. What happens? What goes wrong? Why so much waste? Those are, I think, legitimate questions. I don't necessarily expect answers. Why, too, are so many priests so bad at what they do? Why, for example, is the administration of the sacraments so poorly done by so many of them?

I confess, I have a poor image of priests in part because of what many of them had said falsely about me. But even taking that into account, the present condition of the priesthood is depressing. We desperately need a revival.

Nothing much I can do about that. It's your job and your Holy Spirit's job.
I love You.

August 16, 1999; 8:45 a.m.; Grand Beach
My Love,

Ponsot's poem this morning is about a young aviator her age who was killed in the war, Korea most likely. She sees in her dreams his flaming body falling into the sea. His lovers love someone else now. Only the memory remains, and that fades too, after his mother dies and his name is no longer mentioned at Mass. If he had lived? Well, most of his life would be over by now anyway. That, by the way, as You well know, is my addition to her attack on the brutality of war.

Life is tragic—no way one can escape it. We all end tragically, one way or another. We don't need wars to accelerate the problem, do we?

The answer is neither to deny the fact of death or brood too much on it. Difficult task, especially as summer winds down, a busier summer than I had hoped for. Still, I thank You for life and for all your gifts . . .

And I love You.

August 17, 1999; 8:05 a.m.; Grand Beach
My Love,

This morning the poet writes about memory. A dangerous thing, memory, she says, because it fills our dreams. My dreams the last few nights have been vivid, but somehow I can't remember any of them. My memory continues to be clouded with mistakes and failures. Yet, I have used memories to produce my stories, and so many people find hope and grace in the stories. So my memories must be graceful.

How silly can I be. I guess I'm tired this morning. I don't know why. Capable only of stream of consciousness.

Anyway—and still—I love You.

August 18, 1999; 7:46 a.m.; Grand Beach
My Love,

Five thousand people (at least) died in one of the worst earthquakes in history in western Turkey. I wince at the images, feel terrible pain for their suffering, and wonder why such things happen. Death lurks everywhere, does it not? I need only look at the death notices in the paper with all the American flags denoting veterans to realize that my generation is dying off and that I live, to some extent, on borrowed time. Even if there had not been an earthquake in Turkey, the people would have died relatively soon anyway. There is enormous pain in quick or lingering death, and then grief for the survivors, the lives of many of the survivors destroyed by grief. Then oblivion. Rescued finally by You? Yes, if You are a God worth believing in.

Do I fear death? Sometimes, like this morning I feel (for some reason) that the end of life as such would not be bad, but dying is a painful, sad, tragic event. Pretty morose, huh? Life makes sense, I guess, but only just barely.

Anyway, I accept whatever You have in store for me and will try to be faithful to You, come what may.

I love You.

August 19, 1999; 7:55 a.m.; Grand Beach
My Love,

I finished my final revisions on *A Christmas Wedding* today, ending a thirteen-year struggle to get the first three volumes of this family saga published. Thank You for the success, an event almost as random as the troubles with publishers and agents. I hope the series flies just to prove I was right. There's enough people who liked the first volume to persuade me that the story is fascinating. I hope to do at least three more books—sixties, seventies, and eighties—with your help.

What a fascinating century it has been. The first books go from 1900 to 1960, the earlier decades more sketchy but vivid enough. This could be my masterpiece. Take good care of it, I beg You.

Grim days as a grim week winds down. Then tomorrow I must go in for two weddings, one happy and one, I fear, sad. For me at any rate. Bless and protect those who are marrying.

I love You.

August 20, 1999; 8:20 a.m.; Chicago
My Love,

I had supper with Bill Grogan last night. He gave me the details of Mike's final sickness and death. Horrible! There are no good ways of dying, but some are certainly worse than others. I could die that way or even more horribly. I admit that I am afraid of dying, though not of death. The worst thing that can happen at death is that there be nothing at all, which at least would be painless. The best, in which I believe, is what eyes have not seen and ears have not heard . . .

The painful wrenching of the soul from the body, however . . . That is terrifying. And there is no escape from it. So it does no good to worry about it, does it? Yet, I do, we all do. Again I say, not what I will but what You will. And grant peace and happiness to Mike.

I love You.

August 23, 1999; 8:55 a.m.; Grand Beach

My Love,

Rainy day. Rainy week. Summer is over! Ugh!

As I've said so often (should write a poem about it!)—there's nothing worse than a resort village in bad weather in late summer. Actually, there are a lot of worse things, like the earthquake area in Turkey, so I'm not complaining.

In the face of struggles and hardships, what does one do? Whom does one blame? *You!* Well, no. You know what You are doing—and we simply have to trust You, don't we? I'm sure You will make all things right—eventually. But so many things are wrong.

As You can tell I'm still in the dumps. Existential angst, or as close to that as I ever get.

I must try to be cheerful this week. Help me please.

I love You.

August 24, 1999; 8:29 a.m.; Grand Beach

My Love,

Things are still grim. Weather, family, everything.

But I want to reflect on dogs because of poems in *Poetry* about dogs and a lab on the beach on Sunday tirelessly chasing a prize in the water and bringing it back to his mistress with great delight. Dogs are so much like us that we risk reading human emotions into them. They don't have human emotions, but they do have emotions. They adore us with much more simple-minded faith than that with which we adore You. That's not our fault because You have made us different. Yet, I depend on You even more than that lab depends on his mistress. So what conclusion?

This morning I can't find any.

But I love You.

August 25, 1999; 8:46 a.m.; Grand Beach

My Love,

I'm better this morning, though nothing much has changed. My gloom is, of course, about the end of summer, combined with a week of rain. I feel that summer has been taken away from me by demands that I could not have resisted without great rudeness. The demanders circle around waiting to pounce. Even when I turn down a lot of their demands, they keep circling. Moreover, as I look ahead to the fall and winter, I see the demands increasing.

If I were a retired parish priest, it would be different, though probably not. Yet, as I remarked to Joan last night when she said her daughter was off to Paris for her junior year, it was only yesterday that she was in Florence for *her* junior year.

Time slips by, summer slips by, life slips by. And the demanders circle round still. And I have no time to write poetry—and that's why I'm discouraged. But it's all silly. The gift of life is to be treasured, not clung to. Right?

I love You.

August 26, 1999; 8:24 a.m.; Grand Beach

My Love,

A poet (in *Poetry*) this morning envies the rock and the stream and the current and the trees, that they do not have to worry. He especially envies the wind which sweeps the "earth of windlessness, touches everything and keeps nothing, and is beheld to no one."

Well, yes, that is one way to exist. It is not the way we must live because of your wishes and your generosity. Our way is burdened with grief, tragedy, frustration, disappointment, aging, and death. Also with the obligation to love and be loved—for which we are and must be grateful. Tough business, this business of life—until one considers the alternatives.

The *Wanderer* is telling people that I am dying, a fact that seems to delight them. Well, we're all dying from the moment of our birth. The older we get, the closer we are to death. Then we do die and the *Wanderer* gang rejoices. And that's that—except I believe and hope against hope that it is not that and that we continue.

And I love You.

August 27, 1999; 9:06 a.m.; Grand Beach

My Love,

Yesterday's poem prayer (my own, as You know):

Moon Triumphant

Moon grins complacently
She's shown the world
What she can do
Blow out the sun if she wants

Admittedly time and place predicted
Not here actually, but in Cornwall
Weird rocky Celtic place
Yet even the Pope moon-gazed

Moon graciously bows out
Chastened the sun comes back
Moon has had her day

Last in this millennium

Yet she doesn't scare anyone
With these ingenious tricks
With few exceptions
Superstitious Celts we're not

A rock gets in the way
Of a ball of exploding gas
Big deal, O conceited moon
Not even a surprise

Yet in our depths
Eclipses are a little scary
Awe and wonder persist, beauty too
Which, moon, is why She created you.

August 30, 1999; 8:39 a.m.; Grand Beach
My Love,

I cling to summer like a parent would cling to a dying child. I'm sorry.

This morning Ponsot talks about the exploration that a life involves, mistake after mistake after mistake, nonetheless forming a path. So, indeed, it is with life, with everyone's life. Surely with my own. Because of my long memory and my peculiar sensitivities, I remember the blunders, the misunderstandings, the failures, the flaws, the pain, the falsehoods, the exclusion. Especially, today, when everyone is saying, not without some reason I admit, that fall is in the air.

It's a very negative view of my life and work. Not one of which You approve, I suspect. Consider: our article on the increase in belief in life after death will appear in the *American Sociological Review* in December, a major accomplishment. The people who exclude me from serious sociology, whether in the Church or the profession, will continue to exclude me, to define me out. I should be able to see bravely that it is their loss—but I don't.

On the other hand, I'm not going to stop doing or being what I am—and I hope that pleases You.

I love You.

August 31, 1999; 5:00 a.m.; Grand Beach
My Love,

Couldn't sleep, so I'm up at 5:00—as always when I have to get up early and with a difficult day ahead of me! But I did realize as I awoke that I have become crotchety and crabby in recent weeks, mostly because I have been unable to protect my summer from the demanders. The demands are unfair, but that's all excuse to lose my peace of mind. I'm sorry. I'll try to do better. Help me today, particularly at dinner with the cardinal.

I love You.

September 3, 1999; 10:30 a.m.; Grand Beach
My Love,

Friday of the Labor Day weekend. Summer winds down, even if I am going to stay up here to work on my new novel. Thank You for the graces of the summer. Sorry for the wasted opportunities. Thank You for my surprising friendship with the cardinal.

I realized the other morning in bed that love necessarily means surrender. I must entrust myself completely to You, which I haven't done yet—nowhere near. Complete surrender is impossible, but I must accept whatever has happened to me and whatever will happen as part of your plan and yield to You. Then a lot of my angst will slip away. So I will try this long weekend to accept gracefully the end of summer.

I love You.

September 4, 1999; 8:05 a.m.; Grand Beach
My Love,

Yesterday when I came in from skiing, exhausted but exhilarated as usual, I grew sad because it was probably the last ski expedition of the summer— and maybe the last ever. Will I be around next summer? If I am, will I be able to ski? Now, to be honest, as I must with You, I think those terrible things at the end of every summer.

But what a stupid way to approach skiing and life. I should have reflected that I had a great skiing summer . . . and at seventy-one. How could I possibly complain or lament?

Dummy! And despite everything a wonderful summer! For all of which, many thanks. As for the world to come, there'll be something like skiing there, only better.

I love You.

September 5, 1999; 9:15 a.m.; Grand Beach
My Love,

What a generous parent You are
Creating the various seasons
Plugging in the North Star
All for your loving reasons
It might be summer all the time

Or winter even worse
As the poet says make mine spring
Creation breasts from which You nurse

September 6, 1999; 9:23 a.m.; Grand Beach
My Love,

Labor Day Sounds

Off-shore boats roar
Wave runners snarl
Ski boats thump
Jet planes whine
Lake slushes
Kids screech
Parents yell
Teens giggle
Dogs bark
Sea birds squawk
Quiet day on the beach

September 7, 1999; 9:30 a.m.; Grand Beach
My Love,

Is summer over? Labor Day says it's over. The calendar says it has three weeks to go. However, there is, as they say, autumn in the air.

I am obsessed by summer, You say. I admit it! I am grateful for summer in general and for this summer in particular. Yet, I realize that I have one summer left in my life. That makes me melancholy. I'm sorry.

Why do I think I can escape the human condition? Actually, I don't think that. I merely lament the human condition—but I accept it, not that I have any choice. And so today, I start seriously to work. Grant that it all may be for You.

I love You.

September 9, 1999; 10:05 a.m.; Grand Beach
My Love,

Well, my computer didn't collapse from 9/9/99 bug!

I'm still not doing very well. End of summer malaise. Sorry.

Two mysteries reflected in my recent reading: why anything exists at all and why the cosmos is comprehensible. Work those into the novel somehow.

Are these two mysteries the basis of all religion? I tend to think so. They both suggest grace and possibly (probably, certainly) Grace.

Another mystery is consciousness.

Silly argument against the second mystery is that all is chaos and chance and our world emerged as a result of tiny probability there would be a comprehensible cosmos.

Mystery is renewing—but the cry of the heart is, "Where, in all this vast mystery, is there a place for me?" Or is there one? I believe that I am loved—and that's my place.

Hence I try to love You as best I can.

September 13, 1999; 9:35 a.m.; Grand Beach
My Love,

Back here at the lake after a weekend in Chicago. Discouraged again. Too much running around, too many obligations. Phil has announced his intention to retire at the National Opinion Research Center (NORC). As usual this makes me feel vulnerable. I suppose it shouldn't because it really doesn't much matter. However, that's only a medium-size problem compared to all the others that I experience. Getting back here lifted my spirits a bit. I'm ashamed of myself for this discouragement. I suppose it's related to a sense of mortality. I am ready to die whenever You want me to die. I must get beyond that and continue with life. Please help me.

I love You.

P.S.: Maybe I have too much imagination.

September 14, 1999; 8:34 a.m.; Grand Beach
My Love,

Three major family problems face me, all out of my control, save for the fact that I will be expected to do something about them.

And other worries too, about which You know.

Ponsot has a wonderful moon poem this morning. Makes me want to throw mine away—or try to write another.

I am also so dry, so barren spiritually. My fault, I know. Trying, as always, to do too much. If I should die this year, who would worry about the problems? Who would do all the things I feel I have to do? On the other hand, my life has been so blessed with so many things that I have no right to complain. I must concentrate on my blessings.

Help me to do so and to love You more.

September 15, 1999; 9:23 a.m.; Grand Beach
My Love,

"We all die young," Ponsot writes this morning. In the midst of plans and projects and dreams and unfulfilled yearnings. There is so much more to do but no more time to do it. Our secrets, she says, remain secret.

Indeed, that wisdom fits my mood this morning. I get up. I eat breakfast out of a can. I read the papers. I check the e-mail. I do this morning prayer. I begin to write. I try to cope with all the problems that linger around me. I answer the phone. I make phone calls. I keep on writing. I read at the end of the day. I swim. I go to bed exhausted. Who will do all these things when I am no longer here? Why do I do them now? What would it be like not to do most of them?

I don't know. I trudge ahead because I must. I write because I must. I would like a real summer vacation. All that is foolishness. I have had a blessed life and am grateful for it.

I love You.

September 16, 1999; 8:10 a.m.; Grand Beach
My Love,

My front lawn, which I inherited and which I really don't like, is being destroyed by the moles. That seems this morning the perfect model for my current life: eaten by small problems. Not so small in their reality, but small in my ability to do anything about them. Also, the destruction of the lawn represents the destruction of summer which, in fact, was destroyed in part by the constant trips into Chicago on harassments I couldn't escape. I have gone through this summer-to-autumn change literally scores of times in my life. Now, perhaps for the first time, I'm not sure about the autumn rebound. All I see happening in autumn is an increase in demands as my time fills up.

Can I break out of this rat race—a cliché if there ever was one? I don't see how. As I grow older and feel the need for more time for peace and reflection, the vultures want to take more of my time away from me. Even when I say "no" to most of the demands, I still see my time consumed. Will it ever end? Not in this life, I fear.

I love You.

September 17, 1999; 9:25 a.m.; Grand Beach
My Love,

The characters in the story kept me awake for much of the night. That means I'm really into the story. Almost half done. Back to Chicago again for the weekend. More demands to face. I feel less discouraged this morning.

I didn't reflect on my dream of the night before last. The cardinal asked me to become his vicar general. I declined for reasons of age. Then he begged me, and I agreed. My first rule was that no one works after 4:30.

Could I be a good vicar general? Certainly not. In the short run, like a week, I might be all right. I'd fire just about everyone in the office!

It's not my world, however, and not my fight. Marginality, as I realized long ago, means freedom. And I am free, thanks be to You. Still please take care of him. He's a friend.

I love You.

P.S.: Thank You for sending him to us.

September 19, 1999; 9:10 a.m.; Chicago
My Love,

A very busy and roller-coaster weekend. High point was the liturgy at St. Mary of the Woods (SMW)—which was wonderful. Despite the sad encounter with my sister, Grace, at the nursing home, the Eucharist made me happy. I felt like a priest—a priest who became happy because he was able to make other people happy while he presided over the Eucharist. Thank You for this wonderful experience in the midst of others not so wonderful.

Ought I to be in a parish? Too late now. Probably not. You want me to do other things. I'm glad I can still have the parish experience sometimes.

I love You.

September 20, 1999; 8:45 a.m.; Grand Beach
My Love,

My last week here in Grand Beach. Looking back at the summer, I see another failure. However, I accept failure as part of my limitations and finitude. I tried, and You love me for trying—even as You love me when I don't try.

If I were You, I'd be very impatient with me. You have blessed me with so much. You have given me so many opportunities, and I blow so many of them. Still, You continue to bless me, for which I am grateful. Please take care of me and protect me and help me to improve in my faith and hope and love.

I love You.

September 21, 1999; 9:15 a.m.; Grand Beach
My Love,

The anniversary of my father's death was four days ago. I did not notice because I had lost track of the dates as I worked on the novel. Fifty-two years ago Ed Fitzgerald pulled me out of line after breakfast and told me that my father had been anointed the night before. No chance to call home. No ride home. On the North Shore and then the el. Unconscious at St. Anne's. Dead a day or two later. Back to the seminary. How heartless that system was.

My life changed, as it always does when a parent dies. I never really had a chance to relate to him as an adult. A gifted, honest man who had a hard life and wore himself out early—and smoked too much.

How much of what I am is attributable to him, especially the stubborn integrity. He was a man of honor and respect. I don't think I am but only to those who have turned me into an inkblot.

I will be with him and my mother soon—in your good time. If it be your will, convey my thanks to them.

I love You.

September 22, 1999; 9:50 a.m.; Grand Beach

My Love,

Coming home from the dinner party last night and feeling good from the meal and the splendid conversation, I looked up and saw my friend the moon, glowing and smiling down on me. I suddenly felt that despite all the hassles and failures this summer, it was still a very good summer and I am very grateful for your many gifts and ashamed of myself for complaining. I'm sorry.

This morning I must return to writing the novel, something of which, after the last several weeks, I am very tired. However, it is your will for me and my vocation, my challenge while I yet live.

I love You.

September 23, 1999; 8:12 a.m.; Grand Beach

My Love,

First day of autumn. Time to go home. Will I ever be back at Grand Beach? Maybe. Maybe not. I place all my trust in You . . .

And I love You.

September 26, 1999; 1:25 p.m.; Chicago

My Love,

All human ventures go badly, all human lives go badly, all human lives necessarily end badly. I reflect on this after a difficult weekend. I visited my sister at the nursing home yesterday. She is deteriorating rapidly. I don't think she even recognized me yesterday. What a terrible life she has had. Why? Do You know? I don't. I'm sure You will wipe away all the tears, including the few I almost shed yesterday.

Not a very cheerful perspective on this Sunday afternoon. As you know, however, I am not in a great mood these days. Sorry. Help me.

I love You.

September 27, 1999; 10:25 a.m.; Chicago

My Love,

I feel better this morning. I don't know why either. I hope it's because I have more trust in You, because I've lifted up my eyes and seen beyond my own problems and worries. They are not unreal, but neither is your love. Everything will eventually be all right. I do believe that. Help me to believe it more strongly.

I love You.

September 30, 1999; 8:30 a.m.; Chicago

My Love,

The world is back in order again—kind of. I've found my wallet, and my new credit cards work, so I won't run out of money. I've been upgraded for the trip to Europe. The reason for my stomach problem has been precisely diagnosed. I'm catching up. I would have thought that a week between a return from Grand Beach and a trip to Europe would have been enough. I never learn, do I?

I hope that all goes well on the trip. Please take care of me and protect me and help me to relax a little and enjoy the trip.

I love You.

October 11, 1999; 8:05 a.m.; Chicago

My Love,

Back from a vigorous and exhausting trip to Paris. I tried to write reflections in the midst of all the running but, as You well know, they didn't amount to much. The columns I wrote on the way back were better prayers.

I continue to be concerned about the procedure on Thursday, but less than I was. My future is in your hands and I trust You.

How Catholic a city Paris is and yet how pagan. Not much has changed since Notre Dame du Paris went up, I guess. Yet, I am depressed at how badly the Church has blown it through the years—and still does. It identified itself with the feudal culture and the power of the monarchy, and to some extent still does. At least the fight with the Revolution and the Republic is over. I am also discouraged by the more general thought that so much of the Church's effort has gone into "defending the faith," especially in France, against the Revolution. It would have been much better to have done earlier rather than later what Leo XIII tried—make peace with the Republic. Would it not have been/be better to propound the faith, teach the faith, instead of obsessively defending it? Your Son's promise that the gates of hell would not prevail seems to have put the obligation on himself rather than us.

But what do I know!

I know that I love You.

October 12, 1999; 9:55 a.m.; Chicago

My Love,

I had to bow out of a wonderful performance of Verdi's *Falstaff* last night (with four gorgeous women, a first for any opera I've seen) after the first act because of exhaustion from jet lag. I thought I was doing fine till about 5:30. It's the trip back that does it. Somehow it is a brutally long experience. Maybe I'll rethink my plan to go to Ireland next month, regardless of the outcome of the procedure on Thursday.

I am reading a book on beauty by Elaine Scarry, a book that itself is beautiful. I find that I shy away from beauty, which is clear enough in my moon poems. Beauty compels attention. If I stopped to consider all the beauty with which I'm surrounded, I would do nothing else but revel in it. Then what would happen to my schedule, with which I'm so preoccupied?

I am certainly sensitive to beauty—perhaps too sensitive if that be possible, which I know it isn't. I'm also sensitive to the tragedy that is latent in beauty. I don't like to face the tragedy.

So tragedy and preoccupation, those are the enemies of beauty in my life. I must respond effectively to both.

Help me, O Beauty, ever ancient, ever new.

I love You.

October 13, 1999; 8:00 a.m.; Chicago

My Love,

Tomorrow is the day of the procedure at Little Company of Mary. I spend today finishing a novel. Nice irony, I guess. There is no reason to expect the worst, but in my culture and perhaps in my genes, I do. Silly. My body knows I'm healthy, but I won't listen to it.

Sickness, however, does come; so, too, does suffering and death. If this is the time it comes to me, then I accept it as your will and place all my trust in your love.

In this book of Scarry's I'm reading, she rejects the thesis of the past writers on beauty that there is a transcendent beauty. She otherwise respects and admires their work, but on this point she believes they are wrong. But for what reason, I wonder other than the persistence of the enlightenment zeitgeist. What reason does she have to suppose that her understanding of the human condition is better than theirs?

I believe differently, however hesitantly and uncertainly at times. I do believe and I do trust in your love and that You are revealed by beauty. Help me to sustain that trust till tomorrow afternoon and whatever may come after.

I love You.

October 14, 1999; 12:15 p.m.; Chicago

My Love,

Back from the hospital. I've been bumbling and stumbling around because of the sedative, trying to reorder things from the chaos of last nights "prep" interlude. So, only now, as I am preparing to go out to Old St. Pat's (OSP) for the annual clerical birthday party, do I pause to thank You for giving me a new lease on life. I would love You and thank You regardless of what the verdict was. However, I'm happy to learn that there's nothing wrong with my colon at all, at all. Thank You very much. I will try to do my best for You in whatever years may remain.

I love You.

October 15, 1999; 7:55 a.m.; Chicago
My Love,

Yesterday, while I was waiting for my turn at the colonoscopy procedure, I heard a conversation across the hall between a doctor (who was a bit of a jerk) and a man whose cancerous tumor he had discovered. It was a chilling experience. The same thing could happen to me some day, I thought (though now it seems unlikely). Worse, however, was my feeling of sympathy for the man, whoever he was. I felt his pain, his terror, his incomprehension, his grasping for possibilities, his struggle for understanding from the doctor—who was quite incapable of anything more than a gentle and reassuring voice. Help him and protect him and take care of him.

Life is finally tragic for everyone, but all tragedies are different. Mine was merely postponed yesterday. Mind You, I am grateful for the postponement—and a little embarrassed by my levels of concern, though at least I acted like a man of faith and confidence on the outside. Now I must settle down to the matter of attending to beauty.

Thank You for the new lease on life. Thank You, too, for whatever little wisdom I might have learned. Help all those who are troubled.

I love You.

October 16, 1999; 8:40 a.m.; Chicago
My Love,

Waiting for the procedure was a useful experience. Waiting in a situation one cannot control is always useful because it makes one realize how finite and fragile one really is. Finite and fragile, I surely am, even though I strive to control as best I can the forces that impinge on my life. I must not be reckless—perhaps, in some respects, too reckless—but I must also realize that life is filled with unanticipated dangers and one must live in such a way as to be ready for those dangers when they appear. My record in that department is not promising, is it?

The danger I feared in the waiting room was not there, and for that I'm thankful. Yet, as I face the rest of my life, I must realize that I am neither immortal nor invulnerable.

I love You.

October 18, 1999; 8:35 a.m.; Chicago

My Love,

A cold, rainy morning today. Temperature ten degrees below normal. First time I wore my winter coat. Brr! Beautiful view of the lake from dentist's office—iron gray with a flash of cold sunrise-light on it. Rembrandt or someone like him. You're not so much like it, as I learn in the reading I'm doing about beauty, as it is like You. Gray and autumn can be—and are—beautiful.

Emerald Ball was an interesting challenge to my patience. I was jet lagged and recovering from the colon exam. People were intruding, cutting short my progress, interfering with my attempts to be hospitable to my guests. Nice people usually, but pushy. At one time there were four different assaults going on. I had an enormous urge to sweep them away with a single brush of my arm. Of course, I didn't do that. I must watch such matters, however, and keep my cool. There are prices to be paid, I guess, for trips to the White House.

New novel finished, for which much gratitude.

I love You.

October 22, 1999; 7:45 a.m.; Chicago

My Love,

Coming down to earth after the trip to the White House—not from the trip, which was nice, but from catch-up work yesterday. Why must I catch up after a single day? I have recorded elsewhere my reactions to the White House, so You already know them—as if You didn't know them while they were going on! I understand why they hate Clinton: he's bigger than life, and small people always hate big people. I can catch a hint there of why I have trouble. I'm not as much larger-than-life than the president, but I am somewhat larger-than-life—and that's enough to stir up the envy of the small people. Especially priests. The *Plain Dealer* in Cleveland carried my column about the failure of the liturgy because of priests. I got a fair number of priest hate letters, most of them not attacking the substance of my argument but demanding that I return to parish ministry so that I'll know what I'm talking about. As if I didn't do parish work every week of my life. However, it is an article of faith among the brothers that I don't do parish work. Fortunately, I restrained myself and didn't respond to their e-mail. One should never respond to hate e-mail.

Thank You for the White House experience. The president is a good man. I think my family and staff thought that the trip was more memorable than I did. I have long ago given up on memorable events!

I love You.

October 23, 1999; 8:25 a.m.; Chicago
My Love,

In the book about theological aesthetics I've been reading, there is quote from the German poet Rilke that I found striking. One spring, he says, is enough to convince him of your presence. He's right, of course, but that's a dramatic way of putting it. It strikes me especially hard during this harsh end of October, when the temperature is ten degrees below normal and last night, after the concert, I found myself shivering for the first time this winter. Come to think of it, one Mozart symphony is enough, as is one Prokofiev concerto. One burst of beauty ought to be sufficient evidence that there is beauty and goodness and love. In the transcendental theology of Tracy and Lonergan, in the apprehension of specific, we perceive implicitly Beauty. Fair enough argument.

So if there is never another spring (and I sure hope there is!), I know that there is spring and You.

On this windy, cloud-covered Saturday morning, I yearn for spring (which I will encounter, of course, in Tucson in January!) and I yearn for You. However, since I have had one spring (and many, many of them), I already have You—and for that I am very grateful.

I love You.

October 24, 1999; 4:48 p.m.; Chicago
My Love,

There is one advantage of getting up at four in the morning. One can see, on occasion, a full moon *setting* over Chicago. I don't think I've ever seen that before. It reminds me of Rilke, that it is enough to see one spring! I must write another moon poem! Which reminds me, I must prepare a Christmas mailbox parish newsletter!

Today is the first day in seven weeks that I have had a chance to begin to organize myself here. Not much time because I did not sleep last night and had to nap this afternoon, but at least enough time to do something.

Why didn't I sleep last night? The reunion at CK, which was wonderful, but brought back too many memories of failures and waste and mistakes? Not very cool of me because there was so many good times reflected there, too. I got out quickly, just as I did the last time, to escape the pain. What a creep I am to let the pain interfere with what ought to be the much larger joy.

I love You.

October 25, 1999; 9:10 a.m.; Chicago
My Love,

In my reflections this week I'm going to choose quotes from the book on theological aesthetics, which I read last week. First quote is from Paul Ricoeur:

The symbol gives rise to the thought but the thought always returns to and is informed by the symbol.

Christianity is a life-giving and life-transforming story before and after it is a doctrinal system.

By your grace I have come to see that and live by it. It is so very hard to persuade other clerics, to say nothing of church leaders, of its truth (consider the shabby performance of the European bishops during their synod in Rome). My novels do convey this truth to many people and they rejoice in it. Again, many thanks for that skill.

I really ought not to be pessimistic about anything, much less morose, the way I was over the weekend. It's amazing what a good night's sleep will do! Help me, please, to continue to tell the story well.

I love You.

October 26, 1999; 8:03 a.m.; Chicago

My Love,

The quote today is from a man named Van Der Leeuw; it's not unlike the one yesterday:

No religion speaks in abstract concepts, religion always speaks in myths, the language of image.

Again, I have believed this, if not since my childhood, at least for thirty years. So I have tried to speak in the language of story. Again, I am dismayed by the European synod, which has spoken in unremittingly abstract concepts—and arrogant at that. "We have the answers," they are saying, and expect everyone to come running to them. In fact, they want to turn the Church back to its stance in the years after the French Revolution. It is most disheartening. I fear that there will not be a turnaround in my lifetime. I'm sure Your Spirit knows what she's doing, but these men are fools, dangerous blind fools.

I love You

October 28, 1999; 8:45 a.m.; Chicago

My Love,

The quote about art today is from David Tracy: the work of art shocks, startles, challenges us to recognize its beauty and truth. Not all art, of course. Not even a lot, which currently passes as art, but true art. How can anyone think that it's optional? I don't understand how, despite our tradition, despite our theologians, despite the pope, we still consider beauty to be a luxury we cannot afford. Must we in every generation wrest it away from the iconoclasts?

I am going to try to develop this notion at greater length for my presentations in Los Angeles, presentations that I think are likely to face creeps. Already I am angry at the fundamentalist, iconoclastic pragmatic Catholic enthusiasts! Not good. My presentation must be reserved, laid back, cool. Not easy on this subject.

I love You.

October 29, 1999; 7:45 a.m.; Chicago
My Love,

I saw *View from the Bridge* for the second time this week last night. It was even better.

A classic story of self-deception of someone whose tragic flaw was lack of honesty about his own motives. I wonder about myself. Self-deception is part of the human condition. We all engage in it. I suppose the issue is how much self-deception taints and even destroys what we do. One tries to be honest about one's motives and yet, and yet . . .

The man from Cablevision yesterday said that I was the most influential American Catholic. I cannot believe that. I do not believe it. I don't think I'm kidding myself either. I have some influence but not that much. Do I want such a title? Do I deceive myself about why I work so hard and try so many things? He said that the coat of that responsibility must sit heavy on my shoulders. It doesn't do to tell the truth, perhaps because I don't believe it. If it were true, I hope I would answer the same way.

Yet, I wonder how I might deceive myself—not *whether* I do, but *to what extent* I do and about what? No way to find out I guess, except maybe to watch some of my reactions. Anyway, You love me despite all my self-deception.

And I love You.

October 30, 1999; 9:12 a.m.: Chicago
My Love,

This morning I read Roland Murphy's new commentary on Job. Like everything Roland does, it's absolutely first-rate. I am trying to do this reflection this morning on my new voice-to-paper technology, which seems to be working reasonably well. I'm not sure however, that this will be a good way to pray.

The first lesson of Job is that You are a hidden God. You're hidden and mysterious. You are mysterious, hidden, unknown, and unpredictable.

Nevertheless, You love me, so I love You in return. One can't help but return love.

November 1, 1999; 9:25 p.m.; Chicago
My Love,

Doctor today. All is well. For which, many thanks. I do not know why You bless me and not others with good health. Surely it is no merit on my part, though the doctor says I'm a good patient, which means I do what he tells me to do.

Anyway, as I learned again from reading Roland's book over the weekend, You are both free and mysterious, a lover indeed, but one I should never really try to figure out. Why so much beauty and so much pain? I don't know and will never know—until You explain it to me. But I do know that Love is at the heart of creation, and You are that love. That's all one needs ever to know.

I'm tired now. Long day, and I came home to experiment with my Christmas newsletter and got caught up in it and finished it. So I'll have nothing to do but read the next two days. What a blessing!

I love You.

November 2, 1999; 7:55 a.m.; Chicago
My Love,

Moon Sets Over Chicago at 4:00 a.m.:

Tonight, after 10:00 p.m., the moon will varnish everything
With a brilliance worthy, wherever that is, of paradise (Charles Wright).

> Never before have I seen the full moon set
> Nor her bride walk down the paradisal aisle
> To the far edge of gold laced urban net,
> Somewhere out there near Oakbrook or Lisle
> Or Naperville or other undeserving nest.
> She turns orange as she nears the final mile,
> Perhaps in honor of All Hallows's fest,
> And grins a self-satisfied Cheshire smile:
>
> "At last you saw my enticing splendor
> And heard my nightly captivating call.
> The silent, sleeping city's silly blunder
> To pay no attention to it at all.
> Still it's good of you to watch once this Fall
> Stunned with deserved reverential wonder."

November 3, 1999; 8:05 a.m.; Chicago

My Love,

I read Roger Gould's book on the Paris revolutions of 1848 and 1870, seeking to understand the impact of 1789 on France and Europe and the Church. I have not been successful in this effort, though I now have a model that says that, while the French Revolution finally dissolved feudalism, the Church, which could have reacted either by seizing the opportunities of the post-revolutionary world or by organizing itself to fight it, in fact, chose the latter approach. Only at Vatican II did the Church finally dissolve its attempts to hold the revolution at bay (and keep feudalism alive, at least inside its ranks) and the dissolution is not yet complete. The model helps me to understand: a) the enormous impact of history on us even today; and b) the struggle within the Church.

However, at the end of this particular book, Gould, who argues that the 1870 commune was, in fact, a revolt of the Paris neighborhoods against the central government, reasserts the truth that we are all locals, despite the globalization hype. We are all locals; we are all premoderns. We're all from neighborhoods. Hence, I must struggle to understand even better my own rootedness and what it means to me and to my work.

I love You.

November 4, 1999; 7:45 a.m.; Chicago

My Love,

I read *Hitler's Pope* yesterday, a prosecutor's case made up by a man who had grown to dislike Pius XII because, after two years of study, he had come to know him too well. Not the kind of person who ought to have been pope. Yet, what would I have done in his circumstances? We need a different kind of leadership, though it will take a long time.

I continue to work on my new moon poem, which is about how You try to seduce us with the beauty of your creation and, indeed, by seeing that, in our mode of knowing, there is already apprehension of You. Very clever. I'm trying to notice beauty more and more. It's hard on mornings like the present one.

I reread some of *Furthermore!* today. The part about the Cody end. I still become tense when I relive those days. What an idiot I was to get involved! Still, maybe it's what You wanted me to do. Well, if You did, I'm glad I tried—and if You didn't, I'm sorry. It's a shame I can't figure it out yet. It does give me some sympathy for Pius XII. How do you make decisions in time of stress? I have a sense that I have often messed up such decisions, mostly because I permitted myself to become exhausted. Hard to avoid that, but I'll keep trying.

I love You.

November 8, 1999; 8:01 a.m.; Chicago
My Love,

Am I becoming a curmudgeon? Someone said to me recently that all I
wanted to do was sit in my apartment and read. That hit me because it
seemed to be true. I don't like going out for lunch or dinner; I hate "affairs,"
that is dinners of fund-raising, honoring, etc. I like the opera and the symphony, but it seems that there are too many such things these busy autumn
days. And, as You well know, I detest breakfast meetings. On a day like this,
when I have relatively little to do except morning obligations (and some
preliminary Christmas shopping), I look forward eagerly to curling up with
a book and reading. Protect me, I seem to be saying, from people. Or to put
the matter differently, I feel that I'm suffering from a surfeit of people. I want
to be left alone.

I am, generally speaking, friendly and charming, which isn't easy (I admire
the cardinal's ability to carry it off). All I want is a chance to slow down
sometimes, and there's little opportunity to do that during these rushing
days. I feel that I need to catch up on my relaxing—and I'm not quite able to
do that. I grasp at opportunities to escape the rat race and am offended when
these opportunities are violated. Help me please lest I truly become a stuffy
old curmudgeon.

I love You.

November 14, 1999; 9:25 a.m.; Chicago
My Love,

Six days since my last entry! I've been running like crazy all week—and am
still running without, as far as I can see, accomplishing anything. Breakfast,
lunch, and supper with people who want to talk with me. Christmas shopping, which I suppose is accomplishing something. Often I would think of
these reflections and promise I would finish them before the day was over.
And, of course, I never did. I should do them first thing in the morning,
even before e-mail. It should be easy to do that—but despite the best of
intentions, I never do. Tomorrow I will try again. Please help me.

I love You.

November 15, 1999; 9:45 a.m.; Chicago
My Love,

Today I read some of Milosz anthology of "Luminous Things." All of them
were about remarkable places and beauty (i.e., grace) revealing itself in them:
Greece, France, Hungary. I live in a city that is becoming the most beautiful
in the world. I walked through it yesterday. I see it out the window. I read
about it in the book about cows. In the back of my head there are temptations to think about how its beauty reflects You. But I am too tired, too worn

out, too sleepy to note the glory of the sun rising over Chicago this morning or the sun setting last evening. Yet, You are lurking there with your promise of beauty and love.

Is it too late for me? I hope not, but I must learn to give the beauty of the clear sky and pastel buildings this morning a little more time.

I love You in all your beauty.

November 16, 1999; 8:40 a.m.; Chicago
My Love,

I saw *Dogma* last night and was astonished. Flaky and zany film that it was, it still told its viewers a lot about You—You are incomprehensible, hidden (*absconditus*—the absconded one), strange, playful, and Love. At the end of the film, it was almost as if Kevin Smith ticked off one by one all these truths about You, complete with Alanis Morisette, who played You, doing cartwheels. Appropriate for a God who thought up quantum mechanics and chaos systems. Oh, yes, very playful, indeed.

Blasphemous? Well, surely if it were, it was Catholic blasphemy, David Tracy's analogical imagination run wild, indeed, run amok. But no intention to do harm to You or to religion or to Catholicism and in the service of telling us more about You. I found it a meaningful spiritual experience, and I will say so in my column, even if it does offend some of the crazies. I hope some of the young people who see it and laugh at it are absorbed by the metaphors. That's what art is supposed to do: absorb people in beauty and truth. Thank You for the opportunity to see it and learn more about You.

I love You.

November 17, 1999; 9:00 a.m.; Chicago
My Love,

I figured out this morning that I have lived twenty-six years longer than either of my grandfathers, and eleven years longer than my father. So I'm truly on borrowed time! Part of the reason is that I don't smoke, I'm not—like my grandparents—a chronic alcoholic, and I'm the beneficiary of modern medicine, which started in 1945. Also, I probably have different genes.

This is an interesting thought as I face the absolute folly of the upcoming promotion tour on my memoir. The pertinent spiritual insight is that this borrowed time is pure gift, and I should do something useful with it. I will, of course, continue to write novels and do sociology and give money away and try to pray. What else should I do?

Maybe the answer is "nothing else"—that I am doing too much already and that the pace of my life should change. How often have I thought of that and tried to figure out how to do it. Without success. Maybe it's time to

work harder on that conundrum. Help me to think it through, I beg You.
I love You.

November 18, 1999; 7:40 a.m.; Chicago
My Love,

There was a story in the *Times* this morning about a young woman in NYC who was hit on the head with a brick and whose life and sanity and career are probably ruined. It's a typical New York story, though we have them here, too—"senseless," as they say, violence, carried out by someone who is, in effect, a sociopath. The question is *why*, as it always is, when bad things happen to good people. One response is to say that the attacker is evil. Another is to say that society made him evil. Perhaps there is truth in both responses.

Or the crash of the Egyptian airliner, caused perhaps by the suicide of one of the pilots. Why, one wonders.

Finally, as *Dogma* emphasized the other night, the question must be addressed to You. You do not answer. Perhaps You cannot answer because we cannot grasp your mind. Fair enough I guess. I do know that You suffer with that poor young woman and with those people whose ears blew out in the crash and who died horribly and with their families. You suffer with all of us, so Jesus revealed. Moreover, You still love us and will wipe away every tear.
I love You.

November 19, 1999; 8:30 a.m.; Chicago
My Love,

Yesterday I read a book about life in Chicago in the last century and the first part of this century. It brought back all kinds of memories of growing up, the Depression, my family, and the events and people of the '30s and '40s. Vivid, vivid images, some of which show poverty that I had not realized before.

Life was hard in those days, so much harder than it is today, save for the "truly disadvantaged," as Bill Wilson calls them. My mother and father would not be able to believe the luxury of the lifestyle of their children and grandchildren, modest as it is. Yet, the book filled me with sadness. So much suffering for so many people. Dunning, County, the Bridewell. I am grateful for my good fortune. But life is cruel.

You'd better be good at wiping away the tears.
I love You.

November 20, 1999; 9:25 a.m.; Chicago
My Love,

Among the images that filled my memory when I was reading the book about Chicago is the picture of my mother reaching into her purse for money and trembling when she saw how little was left. This happened often and, even from the distance of two-thirds of a century, the image still breaks my heart. If only I could have done something about it. If only in later years I could have made up for it! I know she is with You now and filled with the joy and peace we all desire, but I am still close to tears over what she suffered.

So many others did too, but they weren't my mother. Still, I feel for them also.

I put up my tree last night and the Christmas decorations and have Christmas music on the stereo. When I think of the money I have spent on Christmas presents (even holding inflation constant), I realize what that kind of money would have meant to my mother. And my tears well up again. I give money away, I shouldn't feel guilty. Only sad.

Help me this Christmas, despite my wanderings in early December.

I love You.

November 21, 1999; 8:50 a.m.; Chicago

My Love,

Last night at 6:00, with 800,000 people hanging around (or having hung around for the parade), the mayor flicked a switch and the Christmas season began in Chicago—a week before Thanksgiving and before the First Sunday of Advent. We must be resigned to celebrating Christmas before its arrival instead of afterwards, celebrating the birth of a child before the child comes, and growing weary and bored after the babe arrives. Oh well, there's nothing to be done about it, as I figured when I put up my Christmas tree the day before yesterday.

The Mag Mile is a sea of lights and so are many of the side streets. I'll go down later today and look at it and perhaps try to write a poem. Also, I must do a Christmas Moon poem, or at least try, though I'm not in a very poetic mood today.

But the lights are on as we wage war against the darkness—and that is good.

I love You.

November 22, 1999; 8:23 a.m.; Chicago

My Love,

I found no inspiration in the lights last night, but I did get a Christmas Moon greeting written for my cards:

Christmas Moon *
(Another song of a lunatic)

May smiling Christmas Moon,**
Shining midnight clear,
Replace indifferent Sun
And bring ebullient cheer
To your Christmas fun.
May she chase all needless fear
With new life just begun.
May Love that's lurking near
Lead those You hold dear,
Each and everyone,
To a luminous new year
On January One

I love You.

* Moon is often imagined as a symbol of Mary, the mother of Jesus.
** Moon is full the week before Christmas.

November 23, 1999; 9:55 a.m.; Chicago
My Love,

Five minutes to ten. I get up in the morning, mutter some prayers, read the papers, do this reflection, cope with the e-mail and the phone calls, and have nothing much accomplished. Such a terrible waste of time!

I realize that the above paragraph is absolute nonsense. It's just the way I feel this morning after a harrowing yesterday.

I'm drugged out today—and there were already fifteen e-mail notes.

And on Sunday the promotion tour begins!

And today, after lunch, I turn to a new novel, about which I am telling no one, lest they warn me against trying too much. The warning is valid, of course. If I am drugged today, it is because I didn't get away from this thing yesterday.

I love You.

November 24, 1999; 9:40 a.m.; Chicago
My Love,

Thanksgiving time, a Puritan feast to replace the popish feast of Christmas, which the papists took over. A good idea. I have much to be thankful for, despite my present sluggishness and dread of the upcoming book tour. I thank You for my life, my family, my fascinating career, my good health, my friends, my talents—and especially your love, which sustains me through all the difficulties I experience, difficulties that are minor compared to what most people endure. I don't deserve any of this, but I am grateful for all of it and ask that You continue to guide and protect me.

I love You.

November 25, 1999; 9:05 a.m.; Chicago

My Love,

More gratitude:

For living in the times I do, so terrible in so many ways, but so wonderful in so many others.

For this country, where my family was able to succeed despite being immigrants, though it took a couple of painful generations.

For all the friends with which You have surrounded me.

For the life I live, which I would never have anticipated and which I do not deserve (but which I will take anyway).

For my good health (again).

For the excitement and adventure in which I have participated, even though I don't travel well.

For Chicago and Grand Beach and Tucson.

And for being able to breathe in and out—and for being alive.

I love You.

November 26, 1999; 8:55 a.m.; Chicago

My Love,

It was a good Thanksgiving, very good in fact. Much more relaxed. Thank You for that. How many more Thanksgivings do I have? Silly question. Yesterday's would have been enough, even if the Bears lost!

I must take life as it comes.

The older kids are becoming more stable—that might be why it was nice. Nora is now not interested in bugs but in the piano, which she plays by ear and on which she makes up her own melodies! At seven! It's fascinating to watch her little fingers roam the keys, producing the sounds she hears in her head. I gather her teacher will play something and then Nora will play it. Such talent! Such a talented family, so much of it, alas, for one reason or another, wasted.

Why does that happen? I don't know. I try to persuade people with talent to use it. They are afraid, I guess. Please, God. Nora is never afraid. She certainly didn't seem afraid yesterday.

Your superabundant grace is everywhere.

I love You.

P.S.: Please, by the way, help peace to win in Northern Ireland tomorrow.

November 27, 1999; 8:15 a.m.; Chicago

My Love,

Peace won a major victory in Northern Ireland this morning, for which, many, many thanks. There's a long route ahead, but it's a lot closer now than it was yesterday.

Life whirls by, the poet says this morning, like a drunken bonfire. When one writes a memoir, one looks for patterns and trajectories, the tracings of (your) providence on one's life. I am convinced that there are such patterns, that your invitations are not random, though I don't know how You do it (in the quantum world, maybe?). However, the drunken bonfire model does offer some useful insights. Life does rush by with frantic intensity. So much to do, so little time to do it, every day and life long. Life careens, races, dashes, explodes. It doesn't make sense, only somehow it does.

These are thoughts I will try to ponder next during my meandering. Help me to keep control of my temper.

I love You.

December 5, 1999; 9:04 a.m.; Chicago

My Love,

I'm back from six days of book promotion, utterly wiped out—as I figured I would be. Why do I do these things? They are an utter waste of time—save perhaps for a priest being in the media, which I guess is nice, but have I not paid my dues at this sort of thing. Never again!

Two wonderful poems in *Poetry* this morning: "No moon/no stars, to guide your way. No light/climb up, get in. Be drawn into the night."

Yes, indeed, but as I have said before, I love your night and your darkness (though I am, as You know, an incorrigible day person and soon grow depressed in the darkness). Yet, there is beauty in the dark. I do not rage against the failing of the light. Rather, I like it and await the return of the day patiently. Sometimes.

You are in the darkness; You are in the light; You are everywhere in love. I believe that. I see You not merely behind the fog today but in the fog and in the rain. Still, I'm glad I'm not at Soldier Field today.

I love You.

December 10, 1999; 8:23 a.m.; Chicago

My Love,

All I can do today is to throw myself on your love. I'm pretty much a wreck, and I have another week of book tour and social rush. I'm quite over-whelmed. I'm sorry that I have not had time for these reflections or for a preparation for Christmas—or for anything. Help me especially to keep my temper through this situation.

I love You.

December 11, 1999; 2:55 p.m..; Chicago

My Love,

I was almost comatose this morning at the TV interview. I know I did badly, or perhaps not as well as I should. Even though I was home from the opera last night at 10:30, I didn't get enough sleep, so I had to collapse this morning for a nap. I feel better now, but still worn and weary.

Only three more interviews, one here and two in SF. Plus all the Christmas obligations this coming week. I have been able to keep my temper but, on the inside, I'm on the edge constantly, ready to blow up. Help me through the weekend and the rest of the week, I beg You.

I love You.

December 15, 1999; 8:03 a.m.; Chicago

My Love,

In the midst of my exhaustion and grogginess this morning, I find myself thinking of poignant things: Sean's new house and how sad it must have been for the original owners to sell it; a young couple with child crossing Chicago Avenue late last night; Christmas weariness on the faces of people on the street. I told You I was weary and I am moved by these poignancies— which are, indeed, moving—because I am weary or maybe because I am old and find life slipping through my fingers.

Not much Christmas spirit in all this, is there? Maybe I can squeeze in a day of recollection next week.

I love You.

December 21, 1999; 8:25 a.m.; Chicago

My Love,

Six days since I wrote one of these reflections—and a lot longer since I was serious about one of them. I'm still exhausted from the tour. I have a bad cold. And I'm off first thing in the morning to the dermatologist who needs to remove a lesion from my arm. Probably not serious, but still distressing. Run, run, run. Even my sleep at night is troubled.

Help me please. Maybe tomorrow I'll be okay again. Please. Also take care of me at the doctor's office.

I love You.

December 22, 1999; 8:35 a.m.; Chicago

My Love,

Nothing much wrong with my arm. Some things burned off. Thank You.

Still tired. Still sick. Still gloomy because of the sweetness of this time of the year and my inability to get with it.

Christmas cards. I read them, stack them up, and eventually toss. They represent acts of love from people who care about me. What a shame that somehow I can't thank them all personally for their love. I send them my card and a couple of my books, but that isn't enough. I'd like to be able to talk to them and thank them personally for their love and support. The least I can do is to pray to You for them.

I love You and all of them.

December 24, 1999 (Christmas Eve); 8:45 p.m.; Chicago
My Love,

I relaxed a little today and read Mark Patrick's book. I kind of absorbed Christmas music and Christmas and Christmas presents. But I'm still sick and it's hard to pray. I offer my sickness to You, knowing that You love me, sick or well. I often think when I'm laid up with a cold that it's all well and good because I know I will be out of it soon and return to my regular alert life. But what if it is my final illness and I can't pray much then either?

That shows how I am still influenced by the old view of You—as if You loved me any less when I wasn't able to pray or pray very much. You love me even more tonight, when I am in a daze, than You do when I am fully conscious. That's what tomorrow's feast means, if it means anything at all.

As happens when I'm ill, my patience is short. I become tense and want to strike out. I went over to Walgreen's this afternoon and felt like slugging some of the rude people who bumped into me or jumped into the elevator before I got out (spilling a shopping bag). I didn't, of course, but I don't trust myself when I'm sick.

Call from Bill Henkel tonight. I have to get out to see him next week if my cold is better.

I love You.

December 25, 1999 (Christmas Day); 9:15 a.m.; Chicago
My Love,

The last Christmas of the millennium, people will say. What nonsense! Christmas is Christmas!

Cool but sunny. Nice day for Christmas. Cheery.

I think I'm getting better, if very slowly. For that, many, many thanks.

Help me to be in good spirits today, though I will be exhausted. Why have most of my Christmases been spent in cars? I don't really understand. Anyway, it's in service of others, which is what Christmas is about.

I love You.

December 26, 1999 (St. Stephen's Day); 8:05 p.m.; Chicago

My Love,

Better today, though comatose in the morning because of the medicine, which is supposed to stop the coughing at night. I won't use it tonight. A little bit of energy returning, thank You.

I am now conscious as I pull out of the cold what a good Christmas it was for me despite my illness. I was loved so much by so many people. I fear I didn't respond as I should. Still, the experience, now recalled and understood, was overwhelming. Thank You very much. It should sustain me for a long time—if I let it. Thank You for all the love around me.

I love You.

December 27, 1999; 8:30 a.m.; Chicago

My Love,

I pray for the repose of the soul of my grammar school buddy Frank Schleck and in gratitude for the arrival of my ninth grand nephew, one Conor Murphy. There are still a few of us micks around.

I love You.

December 29, 1999; 8:55 a.m.; Chicago

My Love,

Better! Much, much better! Still a little bit of the cold but the ennui is gone. The sun is out, the temperature is in the forties and I feel great. Thank You for the return of good health after two weeks of sickness. Each time one gets over a sickness and health returns, one realizes what a great gift it is. Thanks again. I'm sorry if I let my low spirits get in the way of Christmas. However, it was a good Christmas time for me despite the cold.

I have found a new book of meditations by a diocesan priest who has become a Trappist. He says that New Year's Day is a good day to befriend time, to open one's self up to whatever the next year will bring, all the graces You will send. That is a very good idea.

I love You.

December 30, 1999; 8:40 a.m.; Chicago

My Love,

You know what I'm going to do? I'm going to have a party next New Year's Eve to celebrate the real millennium, standardizing for the mistake of Dionysius Exiguus—You being willing of course. The media created this millennium craze and have exploited this craze ruthlessly with all their silly lists and "greatest ofs"—and I was on one of the lists! Now having turned it into a big deal, they've scared everyone with talk of terrorism and computer bugs. So most people are going to stay home.

I'd like to stay home too, because I don't believe in New Year's. I am not at all satisfied that the brain-dead folk over at Com Ed will keep the electricity going in the city. And the terrorists could easily drive a car with a bomb in it into the parking lot and blow it up.

Yet, as the mayor said, we can't live in fear, can we? Even if I am blown up tomorrow night—an unlikely but not impossible event—I will be home with You. This I absolutely believe.

In my current Blackie novel, someone asks him if he ever doubts. His answer is, No more than a couple of times each day on good days.

I love You—and I know You will always love me.

December 31, 1999 (New Year's Eve); 8:12 a.m.; Chicago
My Love,

Last day of the year, much millennium hype. I'm sick of it.

A Christmas card from a priest with a wonderful prayer—I am thankful that during my life I've had more pleasure than pain, more health than sicknesses, more happiness than sorrow, more sunshine than storm, more friends than enemies, and that throughout I have been so constituted as to be able to enjoy the good things of life which have come my way, without grieving or worrying over the necessary disappointments and struggles that attend human existence.

Perhaps there is a bit too much self-congratulations in that prayer (by Mark Oerstle). We all still must die. Yet, with some fear and trembling, I can make that prayer, my prayer.

Thank You. I add my personal Amen. I don't deserve your gifts, your blessings, your love. Pure grace. Help me to use them to reflect your generosity.

I love You.

— 2000 —

January 1, 2000 (New Year's Day); 9:00 a.m.; Chicago
My Love,

Well, my machine figured it pretty easily—that it was the year 2000. The world continued to work, and there were no terrorists yesterday. All media hype.

Sad day. Christmas over. Must put it away till next year. One less Christmas in my life. Tough one because of rush and health and book tour. Idiotic. I kind of feel betrayed. Still much grounds for faith and hope. Still tired. Help me to get over cold and recover.

Article about forgiveness somewhere. Confirms my insight that forgiveness is not once and for all but a lifetime work. Must be renewed constantly. Must try to understand and sympathize with the one who has caused pain.

Well-taken point. My New Year's resolution? Good idea!
I love You.

January 2, 2000; 8:25 a.m.; Chicago
My Love,

All packed for Tucson. I dread the adjustment at the other end of the line.

More about forgiveness and working at it. I have been surprised occasionally when an incident from the past, often the remote past, comes to my mind and I feel the pain of what was done to me, and I grow angry at the person who did it, a person who I thought I had long ago forgiven. I am ashamed of myself when that happens. I do not want to get even with anyone, of that I am sure. If I meet them, I am always courteous and friendly. But the pain and the anger remain. I thought I had put it away, but it sneaks back.

Such events are not all that surprising. One must go through again the original routine of forgiveness, of trying to understand, of being sorry for the other's pain, of resolving that my anger must be damped down if I cannot make it go away. I hope, after the reflections of these days, I will be more conscious of how much still lurks inside me.

I love You.

January 5, 2000; 9:12 a.m.; Tucson
My Love,

Seventy and sunny! How glorious! Thank You!

I'm just about organized and, starting tomorrow, I go on a relaxing schedule.

I must continue to monitor my feelings and my emotions about forgiveness. And back to contemplating, too.

I love You.

January 6, 2000 (Epiphany); 10:00 a.m.; Tucson
My Love,

Today is the feast of adventure and exploration and excitement, the feast of those who take chances, who, as they used to say in *Star Trek*, go where no one has gone before. In a way, for all the cautious and careful tendencies in my personality, I am part of that movement. Or at least more so than most of my fellow priests. There have been some failures, but mostly of outside hostility that I did not expect and would not have dealt with anyway. I am discouraged now because there is simply too much in my life and it looks like it can only get worse.

Thus, I struggle every day to push ahead on my new novel, with distractions from things I don't particularly enjoy. The trivial interfering with the important (which is also fun). I have the feeling that the final years of my life will be frittered away in the trivial, ever increasingly.

And my own mortality is always on my mind. That's natural, I suppose. I make improvements at Grand Beach and realize that I won't have much time to enjoy them. I buy something for the house here, and I experience the same kind of melancholy. Maybe I would do this less if I were not so tired by the running of the last quarter. I know what must be thought and felt about death. When I'm tired, I lose control of it.

Melancholy thoughts. No clear way out. I must live for the present moment and not permit others to take away my peace and joy. Help me, I beg You.

I love You.

January 7, 2000; 8:35 a.m.; Tucson
My Love,

The novel is finished at last—a week late, which is not so bad considering the problems. Maybe it is a little short. Like every one I've finished, I have the feeling that it is not so well done, a feeling that is inherent in the way I work. However, it is a good story, and we'll see what it's like when I revise it tomorrow. Many thanks for the storytelling ability that has brought me so much fun. I suspect that now the book is done, I'll be able to relax. Nothing, nothing at all on the agenda—till the April talks in L.A.

I love You.

January 8, 2000; 8:15 a.m.; Tucson
My Love,

I watched two Kieslowski's Decalogue films last night. Somber, powerful material, Catholic to its core. It is sad that You called him home so soon.

The meditation this morning speaks of the trillions of stars that are of less value than a single act of human kindness. How true! I'm often kind, almost never unkind. Yet, I am not kind enough. I should keep this in mind all the time.

K's films are grim and somber, Polish, of course, and Polish under socialism. He captures all the grimness of that world. And also the splendor that was there. I have no grounds to complain, even if I am getting another cold.

I love You.

January 10, 2000; 9:15 a.m.; Tucson
My Love,

Recently, the question of pets has arisen, both in e-mail and in reading. Are there grounds for hope that animals may survive in your economy of redemption, especially as we learn more about their consciousness? To this I don't even begin to know the answer. I tell people that it is legitimate to hope, because there are no upper limits on your goodness. Or at least we have no right to assume that there is an upper limit. Your goodness superabounds. This I believe, I must believe, I have no choice but to believe. Now all I need is to fill my life with that faith.

I love You.

January 12, 2000; 8:10 a.m.; Tucson
My Love,

I often feel trapped—caught up in an endless cycle of obligations and re-sponsibilities. Sometimes I think it will be nice when the cycle ends, but I don't really mean that. My first week here is over. I rushed most of the time getting organized. Now I'm off to Stanford for a seminar tonight, then back tomorrow for the first class and out for supper. Run, run, run.

Life as a whole seems like a trap. We rush through it blindly and then look back when it's almost over (as my life surely is) and wonder why we rushed, what we accomplished, and whether it was all worth it. That sounds pretty gloomy. I'm sorry if it does. It's the way I feel this morning. I must try to persuade myself that I'm caught up in this big love affair with You and You want me to do all these things and that I should do them with a smile and with joy in my heart.

I love You.

January 19, 2000; 9:30 a.m.; Tucson
My Love,

I watched a film last night about hyper-orthodox Jews, Hasidim, I think. It was scary to see how much their rules and regulations remind one of us in our bad interludes. The film was obviously hostile, but it made me think that the bad things they do, especially to women, are not unlike the bad things we do. They argue quite simply that women are inferior. We are more subtle. We simply blame Jesus for the way we treat women. I don't under-stand how the Hasidim, a religion of joy and celebration, became a religion of rigidity and oppression, or how we who preach the gospel of mercy and love can be so nasty and punitive, not merely at the upper level but even more so in the parish.

It's my religious heritage, a strong and vigorous one. I won't give it up. But I must say that all this business about the Holy Doors seem a bit much just now.

I also continue to have the feeling that I'm deteriorating, especially because of my difficulty sleeping. Help me, I beg You.

I love You.

January 21, 2000; 8:00 a.m.; Tucson
My Love,

Thanks for the second good night's sleep in a row!

I was very angry last night. I came home from the university at the end of the day worn out—and discovered an avalanche of both mail and e-mail, enough to send me into a tailspin by themselves. In each there was a vicious attack on me, one accusing me of anti-Jewishness and the other of pro-pedophilia. Me of all people! Both were based on terrible distortions of some very good work I had done. Sickies vomiting on me. You know what that does to me! Anyway, I am still angry this morning. I sent a polite letter to both of them, correcting their misinterpretations. Nothing more. I must restrain myself from doing more, even though I am still simmering.

Why? I don't know! If you let idiots disturb your peace, you're an idiot, too—so I'm an idiot! Sorry.

I love You.

January 22, 2000; 8:55 a.m.; Tucson
My Love,

Southwestern Writers Conference yesterday. I spoke at the dinner. After a wonderful teenage mariachi band. Most of the folk there defined themselves as writers, which was their privilege, but in fact they were people who wanted to be writers and had not become writers and would not. The "conference" was a way of confirming their identity. I felt so sorry for them. They had come to learn from people like me (and I don't define myself as a writer, as You know) how to write books that will be published, something that can't be taught. There was a melancholy aura to the event—and a lot of characters who would fit perfectly into a satirical novel or short story.

Yet, it seemed to make them happy, give them hope, provide an impetus to keep trying. I realized once again how many people want to write and are not quite able to do so. I also realized that there might have been a potentially great writer among them. Indeed, it is a faith that you might be such a writer that keeps these people going. All most of them want is a break. I got the break without even wanting it, without going to a writer's conference, without taking a course.

I don't understand any of this. I am grateful for my good fortune but, somehow, after last night, it doesn't seem fair. I don't think many of them felt that way.

Anyway, the teenage Hispanics were wonderful.

I love You.

January 23, 2000; 8:55 a.m.; Tucson
My Love,

I am distressed and depressed by the number of violent deaths. ETA has renewed its terror war in Spain. An army colonel was killed. The whole of Spain rose in outrage. Impressive. Meantime, people are dying in Chechnya, and no one seems to care. The Russians, who hate the Chechens, seem to enjoy seeing them die. I think of Seamus Heaney's Nobel speech in which he rejects violence as a means to justice and freedom. He's right, of course. The world is filled with gratuitous cruelty. Terrible.

What can I do about it? Not much. Except condemn it, not that my condemnation does any good. Wipe away all the tears and help the afflicted and the mourners. I see in my own family what death does to those left behind, and I wince.

Please help . . .
Help what?
I don't know.
Help!
I love You.

January 24, 2000; 9:05 a.m.; Tucson
My Love,

Typical Monday morning chaos. How I hate it. My fault I guess.

I worry about too much. I feel threatened too easily. I am aware of my fragility (I don't mean mortality, though that's part of it, I suppose). I feel often like I'm out on the edge of a precipice, cut off from escape, deserted by allies, with invisible enemies lurking in the brush ready to attack. That metaphor describes the way I feel. The issue is whether I ought to feel that way. The answer is that there were times when I should have felt that way, and sometimes did, but perhaps not often enough. Now there is less reason to feel that way and my reactions are overly sensitive. Yet, while I'm not on the precipice any more, I am still vulnerable to various varieties of crazies. There is not all that much to care about anymore. I've won mostly, even if longevity has been my biggest asset.

I love You.

January 25, 2000; 8:00 a.m.; Tucson
My Love,

You are a strange God, let's take that as a given. I saw the film version of *The End of the Affair* last night. Oddly, it's theme was the same as *Dogma:* You are strange, inscrutable, and often absconded. In Greene's book, and in the screenplay, up to a point, You are very different from Kevin Smith's Alanis Morisette. Still, in both stories, You draw with crooked lines. For some reason, about which I will do a column, Neil Jordan fiddled with the end so that Sara is not the saint Greene intended her to be. Still, it was a powerful film. It revealed to me again the enormous influence Greene has had on me and on my writing, even though, like Kevin Smith, my sensibility is not melancholy. *The End of the Affair, The Power and the Glory*, and *The Hint of an Explanation* influenced me theologically more than all my classes at the seminary.

There still remains the enormous problem of your providence. Sara, in film and story, has a personal relationship with You—even though she doesn't want it—which suggests that You deliberately interfere with human events, to the extent of working miracles. I know You do. I absolutely believe that. I think most people do. The question of how You do it without violating the laws of nature is beyond me. But I firmly believe You do. You are not a deist God, not at all, at all

But You do abscond at the strangest times!

I love You anyway.

January 26, 2000; 8:10 a.m.; Tucson
My Love,

A wonderful review of *Furthermore* by Dennis Linehan in *America*. Usually, when I read something written about me, I recoil because I don't see myself in the nasty person the article describes. As I told Dennis, I don't see myself in the sweet, thoughtful person he describes either. Yet, it is nice to read something generous. Maybe it will spur me to live up to that charming image. Maybe, too, if I believe that image is even partly true, I won't be so prone to angry reactions.

Anyway, thank You much for the review and for the joy it brings to those who love.

And I love You.

January 29, 2000; 10:00 a.m.; Tucson
My Love,

God, the meditation book says this morning, is always in the strange and the unexpected. I have been reflecting on that a lot lately, influenced by *Dogma* and *The End of the Affair*. You are unquestionably a strange God, and You like to lurk in the unexpected. I worry about so many things that don't happen, and then must contend with the surprises, good and bad, that happen in my life. I still react badly when the surprise is unexpected, usually an unexpected surprise that is bad. I forget how trivial most such surprises are.

I have a hard time with those Catholic theologians who are so impressed by science that they reduce You to a deistic God—one who starts the process and sustains it but does not intervene. Yet, our experience of You is with One who is present, easily accessible to dialogue, One who needs us, One who loves us intimately and passionately. I don't understand how the latter can be true. Yet, it is; I know it is. I wish we had a better way of explaining it.

However, I should pay more attention to the good surprises in my life. I was thinking yesterday that I should not have felt so exuberant about the *America* review. I really didn't need it, did I? Well, I did—and I'm very grateful for it. It was one of your surprises, and I liked it. You didn't act directly. I never said that You did. But You acted just the same and You love me personally.

How hard I want to try to love You in return.

January 30, 2000; 10:05 a.m.; Tucson
My Love,

The meditation this morning says that love grows with distance and that we need to leave a place to return to it with more appreciation. In a couple of days, I go back to Chicago—a place I love, to people I love. I don't, however, want to go back. I want to stay here. I know from past experience that those five days in Chicago will be a long weekend from hell. I know that the weather will be miserable. I know that people will be tense and then I'll be tense. Blotto!

More demands. More things I have to do. Bah! Humbug, even!

I'm sorry I feel this way. I've just begun after my first month here to adjust to a somewhat more relaxed style of life. Now I must go back into the whirlwind, and an icy whirlwind at that. Brr!

Well, I got that off my chest anyway.

I will, of course, go home, and I will do my best to be charming, to radiate your love. Help me.

I love You.

February 1, 2000; 8:20 a.m.; Tucson
My Love,

Two phone calls, both involving things that needed to be done, during breakfast. As far back as my first year in parish work, I knew that calls during breakfast are a warning that it's going to be a bad day. Ugh!

I find that I often sit down at this computer at the beginning of a day, already tense and anxious, even without the phone calls. I am impatient with the things that get in my way before I can begin the constructive part of the day—phone calls, e-mail, snail-mail, the nuts and bolts of life—even while I am still struggling to wake up. I would so like in the morning just to do nothing, to sit back, read the papers, listen to music, sit outside in the warmth, vegetate. How rarely can I do that!

At this point in the morning, tighter than a drum, I am spiritually dry. My own fault, I guess.

In any event, I love You. Help me to love You more—and to relax more.

February 5, 2000; 9:25 a.m.; Chicago
My Love,

Seventy-two years old. Many thanks for all the blessings. Lunch with Marilyn; dinner with the Martys; Eileen's party afterwards. I'm tired as I expected to be from all the running. I wonder if, at last, I'm running out of energy.

Anyway, I tend to be depressed right now, mostly because I'm tired and partly because the realistic thought comes to me that there won't be many more birthdays. However many more You give me, I will celebrate in gratitude for your love.

I saw *The Third Miracle* today. Not the world's greatest film but challenging to a priest. I'll reflect more on that tomorrow, when I'm less tired.

I love You.

February 6, 2000; 8:30 p.m.; Chicago
My Love,

Sunday evening at the end of the birthday weekend. A visit to the doctor tomorrow which, as You know, I never like till it's over—then back to Tucson. I am in a terrible mood, weak in faith, hope, and love. I'm so sorry. I feel dry, empty, depressed—not a good way to react to a birthday. I'm so sorry, so very very sorry. Please forgive me. Help me to retool when I'm back in Tucson.

I am grateful that I'm a priest. I'm grateful for my life. I'm grateful for my seventy-two years! Please help me.

I love You.

February 7, 2000; 8:35 a.m.; On the way back to Tucson
My Love,

I feel miserable. Not because there is anything wrong with me, but because the nuns at Little Company have fired my doctor, Marty Phee, the pillar of their staff for three decades, because his Parkinson's disease has slowed him down. I told him I wanted him to continue to be my doctor. He could have fought them, but he felt that perhaps it was a message from You, which it might have been. You do use strange messengers sometimes. He has dedicated his life to the service of other people and has been a superlative doctor. His wife is dead, his daughters are scattered (and some of them show little interest in him), he and his "significant other" have broken up, and now the practice of medicine has been taken away from him. 'Tis not fair. I will stand by him. Indeed, with his permission, I will write the nuns to tell them what

I think of them.

My own health is fine, for which many thanks, despite my anxieties that are always ridiculous. Cowards die a thousand deaths . . .

I thank you for the graces of my trip to Chicago, as hectic as it was. Help me to relax for the next month in Tucson.

I love You.

February 8, 2000; 8:15 a.m.; Tucson

My Love,

I'm still shocked by poor Marty Phee, a man who gave his whole life to medicine—and is now isolated and alone. Please take good care of him for me.

I love You.

February 9, 2000; 9:20 a.m.; Tucson

My Love,

Tragedy and comedy, good news and bad news. Good news: the *Sun-Times* is resuming my column. It's been a long wait. Thank You very much. I survived an anti-Catholic attack, mostly because of longevity and partly because the editor had by chance stumbled on my poems. Then the bad news, a horrific anti-Catholic attack on Mike and me by a man we thought was a friend. Same pattern: deep historical dislike and hatred for Catholicism. It will be a messy, time-consuming fight. Outcome doesn't matter all that much, I guess.

Tragedy: Marty Phee, and the death of Bob Collins in an airplane collision. Are these part of your plan? They have to be in some sense. I believe in your love. There's no point in trying to figure it out, however. I struggle, I survive, I win, I lose, I live, I die, I try hard. Why do so many people hate me?

Well, I know the answer to that, I guess. I'm not about to change, I shouldn't change. Help me to be loyal to what I believe—and not get angry.

Grant rest to Bob Collins.

I love You.

February 12, 2000; 7:55 a.m.; Tucson

My Love,

I had the CK dream again last night. A theme returned that I have not averted to before. I am going to start the high club again (after thirty-six years!) but I hesitate to announce it because of the pastor and before I know it, it's October already and (for some reason) it's too late! There's also an eager young priest in the parish, perhaps me, who doesn't know what he's doing, but is a nice guy.

As I look back on those years—which obviously still haunt me—there was so much waste of energy, so much folly, so many lost souls. Now, when I go back, the people who are still around seem to adore me. But that's selective perception. They don't remember how much of a jerk I was, how many mistakes I made, and how everything failed.

Grim thoughts on a grim morning when I feel very old and tired and like everything I have done is vanity and a waste of time and chasing the wind. Yet, Beethoven was wonderful last night, for which many thanks.

I love You.

March 2, 2000; 7:55 a.m.; Tucson

My Love,

Last night I read the papers from the class on the film *Commandments,* which was based, more or less, on the Book of Job. The young people's views were what one might expect from people, most of whom had suffered no deep traumas in their life. We have to take the good with the bad. Since there has been so little bad in their lives, it was an easy answer. But the truth is that I have not suffered all that much in my life. My health has been and still is astonishingly good. My energy level, not as high as it once was, is still pretty high. I'm an inkblot for a lot of people, especially priests—but a source of hope for so many more. I hope that, when sickness and death roll around, I can face them with hope and confidence in your love.

So there is no reason, except weariness and lack of faith, for my present moods. I must be more open to your presence in the world and in my life, and thank You for that, despite all my running around. It is time to look up and live, instead of sinking into Celtic melancholy and reveling in being morose. Help my love to become powerful in my life.

I love You.

March 3, 2000; 8:30 a.m.; Tucson

My Love,

Dreams last night of CK and Pat Gleason, brought back by references yesterday to parish anniversaries. Then this morning, memory images of Jake McAvoy. I know you've been good to both.

I'm twenty years older now than Pat was when he first came to CK. Yet, he was old then and I'm not, mostly, to be fair, because his health was poor even then. That was a strange relationship, one of the many strange ones in my life. Even now I don't understand it. I suppose that, to put the best face on it, we were both caught in a system that twisted everyone and which, to some extent, still does. The name of it is clericalism. Poor Jake, dead now more than forty years. I used to say—and still say—that if one has to be as generous as he was, very few of us will make it. Maybe he was too generous. Pat thought so. His treatment of Jake still horrifies me. I trust that they are now reconciled.

What is the meaning of all this painful nostalgia? To tell the truth, I don't know. Maybe they are unresolved tragedies of my life, not my tragedies but tragedies I have observed and about which I could do nothing.

I don't know, my Love. Things do not arrange themselves well. So much goes wrong that shouldn't go wrong.

I love You nonetheless.

March 4, 2000; 9:25 a.m.; Tucson

My Love,

Why am I not more content with my life, with my role, with my contributions, with the grace that You have enabled me to be?

Because I'm a jerk, that's why! I'm sorry.

You have blessed me abundantly. You have enabled me to reflect You to hundreds of thousands of people. Normally, the danger would be that someone would get a big head from that kind of success. I hardly notice it. I discount it. I let myself become depressed because of it. I seem to want adulation from everyone as a proof of my work. What nonsense.

And I seem to want to live forever.

I must mellow or, to be more precise, learn to act like a wise man, even if I'm not one.

I love You.

March 9, 2000; 8:35 a.m.; Tucson

My Love,

Grace is everywhere. I have encountered the serene warmth of this place many times when I come out of the airport. Yesterday I perceived it as grace for the first time. I was returning from Chicago, which was actually warmer than Tucson (which proves that You really are a humorist!), after a busy two days and the usual hard plane flight. I walked out of the terminal and suddenly felt peace. It lasted through the day and even till now. I seem refreshed and relaxed. It probably won't last. Yet, in a world where such a surprise can occur, there is a point to living and a point to life and a promise of yet more life. How wonderful and how clever of You.

I love You.

March 14, 2000; 8:55 a.m.; Tucson

My Love,

A madly busy weekend—TV crews coming in and out, each for a different purpose. I think I did pretty well. There was also Mass and a lecture at OMOS.

So today, Tuesday morning, I'm sleepy and lazy. I will not work after lunch today. No way.

I have paid little attention to my TV role. It's a time-consuming nuisance. Yet, it is also, if I stop to think about it, a grace, a chance to talk about You and about the Church in a way very few priests have. By your grace, I do it pretty well. Even June Rosner was pleased with my interview yesterday with Bryant Gumbel about the pope's penance service for the bad things the Church has done in the past. Long overdue perhaps, but still a turning point. We no longer have to defend every damn fool thing a pope has done. Next step will be an apology for all that we have done and still do to our own people.

The next couple of weeks are going to be fiercely busy. Help me to stay close to You during them.

I love You.

March 15, 2000; 8:25 a.m.; Tucson
My Love,

In the poem this morning, the author (male) tells about washing wine glasses in the sink and describes it as "the gray sacrament of the mundane." What a lovely line. There are so many sacraments of the mundane all around, by no means all of them gray. I look out the window this morning and see hummingbirds against the blue sky cavorting around an octillo tree, striving to come alive after last week's inadequate rain. You lurk there and in the wine glasses and in every other marvel of creation, if only I would take the time to see them and be open to them. In the rushed days ahead I so much want to be open to You.

Help me to love.

March 22, 2000; 8:45 a.m.; Tucson
My Love,

The last two days have been disasters. Yesterday I intended to start with my reflection, but the computer intervened with its two-week virus warning and I never got back. Both days was run, run, run all day. And I'm here in Arizona! If I die of a stroke it will not be because of sociology or fiction writing or even air travel (I am grateful that I bounced back quickly from the D.C. trip), but from mail, phones, and e-mail. There was nothing in the two days that could be eliminated. It was all obligation.

I love You.

March 26, 2000; 9:15 a.m.; Tucson
My Love,

Sunday morning in the desert and I'm tired and depressed; tired from the jet travel—of which the worst is yet to come—and depressed from thoughts of mortality. In his intro to the poem I read this morning, Milosz says that it is one of those "everything is all right" poems, a description of a splendid, peaceful, spring setting. I know it well. I could look out the window and see it now. But in my weary old soul, there is no sense of peace or beauty. Just exhaustion, frustration, the feeling that all I have done has been wasted, no matter how good some of it may be.

Another sex scandal may or may not break in Chicago. If it does, I will be blamed for dragging up old events. If it does not, I will be blamed for spreading rumors that are not true. Either way, I lose. Well, so what. As someone said to me on the phone yesterday, the blood of the innocent scream for redress. I have no regrets.

Grant however that there will finally be peace and truth.

I love You.

March 27, 2000; 8:10 a.m.; Tucson

My Love,

A lot of activity around my rosemary bush this morning. Gamble quail back at last, a bevy of red-crested birds, chipmunks, and a busy little lizard. It is spring now, isn't it! I guess I didn't notice the change last week, I was so busy running around. The prickly pears have fruit again. No sign of the saguaro blossoms, however.

All in all, quite a show. Life flows again in the desert. Odd life, but surviving life, a life that reflects your persistence and determination in sustaining life. No proof of anything, just a sign—but signs are all that believers need.

I love You.

March 28, 2000; 8:40 a.m.; Tucson

My Love,

The poet this morning recites the poignant line "O my dear child, what will the future bring! It's fall, nature is dying. The little girl is small and frail."

She will die, of course. Horribly, perhaps, like many of us. The father senses that and he would protect her if he could. But he cannot. No one can. We simply have to trust in You to wipe away all the tears. What more can anyone say. I see little kids running and playing and wonder how many of them will have terrible lives, ruined especially by terrible marriages.

I shouldn't think about those things, I suppose. It's what comes of being a storyteller.

I also tell the story that your love is stronger than death. I must cling to that story, come what may.

I love You.

March 29, 2000; 8:20 a.m.; Tucson
My Love,

I leave for London tomorrow. Don't want to and yet am still looking forward to it.

Why does my time in AZ wind down with such exhaustion? Should I not go back to Chicago relaxed? I guess not.

Life winds down . . . and when it is all over, I can finally find peace. Too much, too much. Yet, it's never been dull. For that I thank You.

I love You.

April 5, 2000; 8:50 a.m.; Tucson
My Love,

Back here, exhausted. Not so much by the flight but by restless nights. More later—I hope.

I love You.

April 6, 2000; 7:50 a.m.; Tucson
My Love,

Better today, much better, thank you!

I wonder about the theodrama that Barron talks about in his Lenten sermons. Everything is part of your great drama. I am a bit player in it and should give myself over in trust to You. But even bit players worry, don't they? I shouldn't worry. No matter how much of a mess I am now, You still love me. I can but throw myself on your love in all my confusion and weariness and imperfection.

I watch the silly little lizard who bounds around outside. You know about him and love him—at least if your Son is to be believed, and, of course, he is! Why You created him, why You created me, why You created anything at: all are mysteries beyond my dull mind. However You love him and however You love me, how much more You love me according to Jesus. I will not have lived and died in vain—and that's a good thought to hang on to as I prepared for this dubious trip to Los Angeles.

I love You.

April 9, 2000; 8:30 a.m.; Tucson
My Love,

Chicago, London, Los Angeles, Chicago—the last four Sundays. No wonder I'm tired!

If positive reinforcement meant anything to me, I sure had enough of it at the Anaheim meeting—for which I am grateful. Why it means so little is a puzzle. Perhaps because it is not unanimous. Anyway, I'm very tired.

I love You.

April 14, 2000; 8:05 a.m.; Tucson
My Love,

I packed yesterday and am now ready to go home on Sunday. I feel very sorry about it. It's hard saying goodbye to friends and colleagues. Moreover, I cannot help but feel that my time here was wasted. It slipped through my fingers with nothing much accomplished and a spiritual life that was a joke. I'm so sorry. I know that You love me even when I am empty and dry. I know You love me now. I hope to turn Holy Week into a time of reflection and recollection.

I love You.

April 15, 2000; 8:10 a.m.; Tucson
My Love,

The world is filled with death this morning, as reported by the calm, slightly bored voice of the BBC news broadcaster we now have here in the mornings. Meningitis in Niger, explosions at the Kinshasa airport, starvation in Ethiopia, riots in Bolivia. A young man in New York, saving his dog from traffic, is run down on the street . . . Why, I wonder foolishly, as I read Martin Rhys on the six numbers that are a pattern for our universe.

I don't know. I don't know anything. I'm worn out, discouraged, depressed.

On my way back to Chicago tomorrow. Protect me on the trip and on return, I beg You.

I love You. I don't understand anything, but I love You.

April 19, 2000; 7:40 a.m.; Chicago
My Love,

Back home. Four days of fog. Tired. Depressed. Discouraged. What woeful routine! Life has lost all its savor. I go on out of force of habit, but not because anything is exciting or fun or rewarding. Even though the mail about my stories continues to be good, that does not seem to make any difference. I've got to snap out of this. It's been going on too long. Holy Week is the time to do it. Help me these next couple of days.

I love You.

April 20, 2000; 8:03 a.m.; Chicago
My Love,

Seven last words at Rockefeller last night. Went well. Terrible rainstorm all day and then fog. Even worse storm last night. Aimed directly at Hancock Center!

Dead tired this morning.

Retreat starts about noon.

I love You.

Later

I've been doing spiritual reading all day and benefiting from it, especially from a book by Marie Heaney about writing that sustains one spiritually. I can't think of any passage that sustains me except "I do not call you servants, I call you friends"—which may be enough. Another book asks me to reflect on my images of You at various times in life. My earliest images are of awe and perhaps terror. Then You became something like my father, admirable but distant and demanding; then a co-worker in the life of the Church, one who expected major effort from me; then a loving and merciful God, a good friend, a consoling spouse; finally, a vulnerable God who needed me. All of these images have built, one on top of the other, and none has disappeared. They are not logically consistent, but in imagery of You who can be logically consistent? You are also as a lover and a spouse, ready—indeed eager—to hear of my problems and woes as well as my achievements, such as these might be. My God sonnets summarize my images of You. The one that is thinnest, if You will, is of You as vulnerable. I know that's true, but it's hard really to think that the one who is behind the Big Bang really needs me. Yet, on the basis of what You say about yourself in the Scriptures, You are.

Of course, the God of *Contract with an Angel*, which not a single Catholic critic has noted, is my favorite, most concrete (You should excuse the expression) image of You.

Now some quotes come to me:

> God is nothing but mercy and love (Thérèse).
> The kingdom of God is about a foot higher than a man's head (Kerry woman).
> He has need of us so that if one of us should disappear, he would die of sadness (Paul Murray, O.P.).
> The Irish priest who compares You to a mother cleaning up the house for her child's homecoming.

Not bad images and not bad sources.

My biggest spiritual problem, patently, as Blackie would say, is exhaustion, weariness, overwork (as demanded perhaps by earlier images of You). I need interludes like these days when I can, as it were, stretch back, reflect, and pray.

Thank You for the grace of the day so far. Now off for Holy Thursday at SMW.

I love You.

April 21, 2000; 1:30 p.m.; Chicago
My Love,

I suppose today illustrates nicely the problems I have with a reflective life. I had to preside over a para-liturgical funeral this morning because no Mass is permitted. To begin with, that's an absurdity. Exceptions should be made for funerals. The diseased was a man with whom I went to the seminary, so there were lots of memories. I think I did a good job, for which many thanks. However, this was supposed to be one of my retreat days. Only now—1:30— have I been able to return to my state of recollection. I could not turn down the funeral—and I did not want to, but I did want to pursue my recollection. Well, You understand and love me. What more can I say!

Another reflection on my image of You:

As I said yesterday, You are the God of the Big Bang, a remarkable, clever, and resourceful God, with a sophisticated mastery of higher math and the ability to put all of this together with tiny bits of string and particles that no one can see. It is a very impressive trick. How can a reality like You care about me, much less be vulnerable to me? Yet, You say that You are—and I take your word for it, but I remain puzzled. And then, why is there suffering, if You are so clever? That's a silly question, isn't it. That question doesn't impact on my faith, but perhaps only because I have not had to suffer much.

My images are more complicated, maybe because I've read so much cosmology. I don't know what to make of all of this, but I do know I must strive to be more aware of You, more conscious of your presence, more aware of my utter dependence on You.

I do love You.

April 22, 2000; 1:57 p.m.; Chicago
My Love,

I was overloaded with imagery yesterday—the city, strange and ominous in the fog and clouds, then glitter and bright as it is today (and how beautiful it is and how good it is to be home). The agony on Frank Shulteis's widow's face, the smiles when I mentioned Kush's summer camp on the lake, the pain on the face of the cleaning person who told me that her daughter in Poland had died of leukemia (what powerful Good Friday images), the poetic images that poured into my head from the poems I had been reading.

Overwhelmed would be a better word than overloaded. I find that I shy away from some powerful images because I cannot cope with their emotional demands. I want to capture them in poetry, but there are so many of them and they are so strong and I have so little time.

I do believe, however, that the glittering city today is a better image of reality than the fog of yesterday. I think I'll try to write a psalm.

And I welcome a new image of You: "I was in the void and found it suffused with love."

A Psalm for Passover/Easter

I praise You in the vanished fog
And our unveiled, radiant city
I praise You in the child's wide-eyed awe
And a rosary in trembling, aged hands
I praise You in the *Pange Lingua*
And the quiet of the empty church
I praise You in the fresh water
And newly studded candle
And their merger in passionate love
In the brimming glory of the Exultet
I praise You in little girls in pastel finery
And their mothers in Easter hats
In triumphantly bursting lilies
In yummy Chocolate bunnies
And, yes, multi-colored eggs
I praise You in emerald lawns
And blooms of tulips and daffodils
In the warm words and glowing smiles
Of your people after Mass
I praise You most of all because
You are risen indeed alleluia!

April 24, 2000; 7:15 a.m.; Chicago
My Love,

The rain yesterday wiped out the point of my psalm, but still it was Easter and everyone was happy, even though they complained about the weather.

Today I want to thank You for raisin bran, indeed for raisins, one of your most clever tricks. If there are raisins, there has to be You. Well, that's a shorthand argument, but it will do as well as most others.

Some of Walt Whitman's poetry in Milosz's book this morning. He compares the face of a dead soldier to the face of Jesus. Striking image. And true. You died when Jesus died, and You also died when that soldier died in the Civil War, because he was one of your children. So too, as Jesus rose, so will that soldier—and the rest of us. This I do believe.

And I love You.

April 26, 2000; 9:25 a.m.; Chicago
My Love,

Silence, solitude. How wonderful they are. In fact, for all the good (if short-term) impact that my mini-retreat had last weekend, I'm never going to make much spiritual progress in my life unless I have more solitude and silence. I always say, maybe at Grand Beach this summer. And I always blow it. However, I must establish a program of solitude. One day a week? Wouldn't that be cool. No distractions, no papers, no e-mail, no TV, no radio. Just silence. I'll try. Help me.

I love You.

April 27, 2000; 8:00 a.m.; Chicago
My Love,

I wanted to weep when I visited Bill Henkel today. There were so many memories, and his present loneliness and frustration were so sad. It is terrible to see those one knew as a boy become old and infirm. I'm glad I went to see him. I wish I could do something more for him. I resent what age does to all of us—and will do to me eventually—and I trust everything to your love.

I love You.

April 28, 2000; 7:30 a.m.; Chicago
My Love,

Packing today for the first trip to Grand Beach. Only an overnight, but a good idea to go up there and get the lay of the land and also to spend some time during the weekend reading. I am determined to make the most of the summer this year.

The lesson I garner from the poems and the readings this morning is that nothing is ever wasted, not even a scrap of paper on the floor that I pick up and put in the wastebasket for the sake of neatness, not even a rock on the beach that a small child picks up and throws at the lake. That is a hard concept to grasp. If You are who and what You seem to be, it is doubtless true. You leave your footprints everywhere, do You not? However, I wonder what kind of being it is that can pull off a trick like that? I suppose that if You launched the Big Bang, heck, You can certainly attend to everything and leave your footprints everywhere. It is the magnitude and the finitude of all these events that stagger my imagination—which is what they're supposed to do!

Hence, You are everywhere and in everything, not only sustaining it all in being, but present, revealing yourself and inviting us to Love. That is truly staggering. Nonetheless, I believe it. How indeed could it be otherwise?

I love You.

May 1, 2000; 8:05 a.m.; Grand Beach
My Love,

Drizzly day. Nice day at Grand Beach yesterday. Nature struggling to be reborn, not making a very good job of it.

Selflessness is the theme this morning, the absence of fixation on self. Yet, even mystics get tired, as I am (aided by allergy pill). I think first of all that selflessness is a joke when applied to me. Then I think how service-oriented my life has been; I think of the tons of e-mail I respond to and the help I give others. I am selfless, sort of, but still preoccupied with myself and my fears and my hopes and my sorrows and my disappointments. I think sadly how much of my life has been wasted in foolish efforts and failed projects.

See what gloomy Monday does to me?

Anyway, I love You.

May 3, 2000; 9:30 a.m.; Chicago
My Love,

I'm struggling through these days without much energy or enthusiasm. I need a long time of doing nothing.

The dermatologist sliced off parts of my skin yesterday. Nothing serious. Thank You for dermatologists.

Nice review in *Commonweal*, not very intelligent and somewhat careless, but generous. I don't usually get that kind of review.

Hard to pray, though I'm working at it. I need Grand Beach with nothing to do but read. Not in the best possible shape to head off to Portugal, but I'll survive. Help me.

Despite my weariness and ennui, I love You. Help me to love You more.

May 4, 2000; 9:45 a.m.; Chicago
My Love,

Off this afternoon to Lisbon. I'll celebrate my forty-fifth anniversary in the priesthood there, far from home as is often the case. I'll miss the class affair, which is all right. I don't much care. Images flow back through my memory of the ordination day itself: cold, happy, family, bright promise, uncertainty, confusion, hope. I could not even have begun to imagine what would happen in my priesthood. I could not, indeed, even imagine the changes in the Church, in the country, in myself. Talk about surprise! I am deeply grateful for your call to the priesthood, for the challenges of my ministry, for all that I've learned, for the excitement, the adventure, the surprises— especially the surprises. They continue even to this day. If I complain often, let it be clear that I know, deep down, that I have no reason for complaint. Help me to continue your Spirit wherever she leads me.

I love You.

May 12, 2000; 9:00 a.m.; Chicago
My Love,

Back from the Lisbon meeting and exhausted—with either a cold or bronchitis. I'm sure that You don't need to hear anymore of my complaints this morning.

Ed Egan is the new archbishop of New York, and John Piderit is stepping down at Loyola. As my sister says, why do You let such things happen? You leave us our free will and You let people develop power bases and others fail to counteract them. So much harm done to the Church and its work and its people. No one should base his faith on a new archbishop. But many people, not understanding what a religious heritage is, can't distinguish between the essence of that heritage and the men who exercise authority within it. It makes life so much harder for the rest of us.

My work on Russia was well received in Lisbon. Nice people as always, but the process is not free from the narcissists. Maybe it never will be.

Right now I am too discouraged to think about anything. I may just go to Grand Beach and do nothing at all, even if I have a novel I should finish. I feel dry, empty, and old—again.

But I still love You.

May 13, 2000; 8:10 a.m.; Chicago
My Love,

The city is beautiful this morning—glowing emerald and sapphire in the light of the sunrise. The lake and river gleam, the trees and grass are exuberant in their youth. Spring's vitality everywhere in the midst of this merry month of May.

I, on the other hand, am devoid of vitality. Is it jet lag? Is it a cold? Is it bronchitis? I don't know. I'm almost to exhausted to care.

We are all called to be contemplative, Brother Wayne says this morning. Doubtless that is true. I have tried, but I am so caught up in illusion and delusion that I have never made much progress. And that very model of making progress is itself an illusion and a delusion. No wisdom for most of my life and now, with perhaps a bit of wisdom, too tired to do anything about it. Maybe I'll pull out of this slump. Or maybe I won't. I feel that my life has slipped through my fingers and I've wasted it in vanities. I'm sorry.

But I do love You, despite all the waste.

May 14, 2000 (Mother's Day); 7:30 p.m.; Chicago
My Love,

A lot of Catholic imagery the last couple of days: First Communion yesterday at SMW, Mother's Day today (with May crowning imagery) at OSP, and college graduation at Loyola. All very lovely. As long as the Church can do these rites of passages well, as it still does, then it has a future, even if dips like Alpine Ed are made cardinals. At the last named, they gave me an honorary degree, which was nice. As my sister said, it was lucky I got it this year because after John leaves, they won't give me the time of day.

Sometimes I think that the history of the Church is a long story of the struggle of the heritage that produces May crownings and First Communions against the leadership. So I guess it must be if leaders are humans.

Somehow, after a good night's sleep and a lovely day and the wonderful sacramentality and a nap, I feel upbeat again—for which many thanks.

I love You. Help me to revel in the treasures of my heritage.

May 15, 2000; 9:30 a.m.; Chicago
My Love,

I have a yucky cold—all I need now. Help me to be pleasant to others despite how rotten I feel.

Why colds anyway?

Mother's Day yesterday and I saw the film *Frequency,* about contact across generations on an old ham radio. Made me aware of my own parents who are with You, yet about whom I never think. Let the dead bury the dead? Too harsh. There is not enough time in my life to think about them or about anything else. Always racing. I think of You and of them and all they did for me. I hope eventually we will be able to straighten it out.

The strongest point in my reading today is the need not to judge. Brother Wayne remarks on how shocked he is about the judgments priests and nuns make about one another. So sad. I don't do that, but I still judge too much. From now on, I'll try to do that. Minor intention, but all I'm capable of now.

I love You.

May 19, 2000; 8:45 a.m.; Grand Beach
My Love,

The weather is still terrible, as it has been since I came home from Tucson a month ago—cold, gray, and rain. As usual, it contributes to my depression, especially up here where spring runs riot because of a few warm days and no one has tried to contain it. My cold seems more or less to have vanished, save for a cough and weariness, which is probably not the result of the cold. I wonder if I am tired because there is something (relatively minor) that's wrong with me or simply because of a combination of age and too much work. In either case, I may have no choice but to relax this summer. Help me to do so. Already people are eating away at my time. They don't understand.

More complaints, huh? As I reflected yesterday, even if I didn't write it down, I have been blessed with excellent health for most of my life (we won't take issue with You about my sinuses and inner ear!) and have lived a lot longer than many of my male ancestors. You have been good to me, granted me a good and exciting life. And then I go into a tizzy because of fatigue, most of which is my own fault anyway. I'm sorry.

I will not live forever; no one does. I do believe, however, that You will give me another life that will be even more exciting than this one. I am in no hurry to get there, but I will try not to be afraid of it when it comes.

I love You.

May 21, 2000; 7:55 a.m.; Grand Beach
My Love,

Everything is green as the sun comes out and paints the environment spring, lush, thick, powerful green. My uncut lawn looks like a field of blooming hay. The foliage seems to close in. The garden has run amok. Life abundant and superabundant everywhere. Life wins again.

I do not draw a philosophical conclusion from this phenomenon. One might say, "How does one dare speak of the Transcendent from a season caused by the wobble of the sun in a small planet in an unimportant solar system in a minor galaxy?" Spring is not a proof in the philosophical sense. Rather, it is a sign, a hint of the underlying dynamics that govern the exploding universe, a suggestion of the enormous and persistent strength of life. It is enough.

How many more such springs? I go with Rilke: one is enough to confirm my belief that You are life and love. I try to slowly slip into the rhythm of spring and summer. I endeavor to leave behind the rush, the haste, the hurry, the hassles, the harassment. It won't be easy. It never has been. But this year, with your help, I will slow down the engine.

I love You.

May 22, 2000; 9:20 a.m.; Chicago
My Love,

It was really hard to leave Grand Beach yesterday. I felt fine up there. Now, back in Chicago, I am harassed and weary again. I suppose, when I settle in at GB, it'll be the same.

I must learn more about humility as Brother Wayne says today. But right now I'm too sleepy to think about much of anything.

I love You.

May 23, 2000; 9:45 a.m.; Chicago
My Love,

Brother Wayne says that humility is the recognition of one's limitations. Let's see what projects I'm involved in. I'm working on a novel and thinking about the next one. I'm engaged in analyzing the ISSP data. I'm writing my three different columns. I did my homiletic web page entry for June. I'm guilty over not doing my newsletter recently. I'm answering my e-mail parish.

Too much? Oh, yes. Why? I don't know! I'm not You. I can't do everything. Yet, I try. And I ask myself why I try. I don't know, I don't know. Should I stop some things? Yes! Which? I don't know. Small wonder I wake up groggy in the morning. Am I addicted to work? Probably. Some things have to go. I don't have to prove anything to anyone, least of all You, who love me beyond my wildest imagination.

I love You.

May 24, 2000; 12:51 p.m.; Chicago
My Love,

I woke up truly groggy this morning, as though I had been drugged, when in fact it was the first night in a long time that I didn't take cough medicine. I'm fine now, thank You, and also thank You that I don't need the medicine anymore.

I have an exciting life, one for which I'm deeply grateful. Maybe I overdid things a little yesterday and had a hard time sleeping, which is probably why I was groggy. But better a day when you have a lot of things to hold your interest instead of a day when there's nothing exciting left in your life.

I love You.

May 29, 2000 (Memorial Day); 9:48 a.m.; Grand Beach
My Love,

Prayers first of all for the young men who have died in war—all of them, regardless of which side. There was a moving article in the *Trib* this morning about how an American had returned to the Japanese family a flag his step-grandfather had taken from the body of a dead Japanese soldier. The Japanese were a fearsome, indeed fanatical enemy in the war. The rape of Nanking and the Bataan Death March were all real events. Yet, families still grieved for their young men who had died in a needless and foolish war. I pray for all of them, regardless of how unimportant my prayers when measured against all the deaths.

I am in one of my agnostic moods. I read a theologian's comment the other day that said if your dog notices you when you come into the house, why do you think God doesn't notice you? The answer is that the dog doesn't have anything else to do, and You, should You exist, are busy with the Big Bang and other such things. Moreover, if You do notice us, why do You permit so many young people to die in useless wars? Why do You require that all of us die, many of us horribly?

Our answer is, for all practical purposes, blind faith in g(G)oodness, regardless. Okay, I make that leap of faith, especially on a morning when the sun finally comes out. Still it's a hard saying.

The point is not that I don't believe in You or love You. I do. The point is, rather, that for some reason, my own mortality among others, I see the difficulties in faith today.

I repeat: I do love You.

May 31, 2000; 10:05 a.m.; Grand Beach
My Love,

The weather continues to be terrible, humid, gray, dismal. Fits my mood. No, maybe it *causes* my mood. Anyway, I must plunge back into the novel, which I don't want to do. It's not that I dislike the story—only that today I dislike the prospect of working. I would much rather curl up in a corner with a book and ignore all responsibilities. Anyway, I won't do that.

And I love You.

P.S.: What do mystics do on days when the weather knocks them out, when they're sleepy, and when they have four thousand words to write?

June 1, 2000; 9:23 a.m.; Grand Beach
My Love,

A new month, hopefully drier and sunnier than the last. Still. I thank You for all your blessings, for the resurgence of my health, for the lake and the beach, and for the progress on my new novel—which now is fun.

As I write about the Vietnam War, I realize once again the Greek tragedy of it. How does human pride impel us into such follies?

Heal the wounds of all those who suffered during those years.

I love You.

June 7, 2000; 8:25 a.m.; Chicago
My Love,

Six days since my last reflection. Sorry. I've been running. Life is difficult right now. Monday I had breakfast with the doctor who is retiring and lunch with the president of NORC, who is also retiring. I don't like wakes.

The last report from the doctor was good. My health continues to be fine, for which I am very grateful to You.

I do know that I must get to Grand Beach and stay there. I feel like I'm trapped here as I strive to touch all the bases I must touch.

Spiritually I'm dry again. My own fault for not squeezing in more prayer. I'm also trying to work on the novel in the midst of all the rush. I want to finish it by the end of June. Right now, it looks like I will. I sense that it's

coming along pretty well. Alas next week is pretty badly cut up.
I love You.

June 14, 2000; 9:30 a.m.; Chicago
My Love,

I'm in the final run-up to a conclusion of my novel—80,000 words before today is over. You know what I'm like at this time, since You have seen it often enough. The characters obsess me day and night, hound me, distract me, keep me awake. That's why I simply must rush to finish. I know You understand, though You don't seem to have been in any hurry when You were creating things. On the other hand, You are God, and You didn't have to hurry!

One day-trip to New York. Useful. Dead tired. Rude to couple that wanted to sit together on the plane and take away my aisle seat. I apologized to them later. They were very gracious. Dumb, dumb, dumb. Sorry.
I love You.

June 20, 2000; 10:30 a.m.; Grand Beach
My Love,

Midsummer's day. The novel is finished. I'm back in the land of the living. Thank You for the grace of telling the story. I hope it's worked out well. It is good to be back to my regular spiritual exercises. I know You understand why it was necessary to throw myself into the story.

Heavy day, driving rain. Longest day of the year, but not much light. Still, we have six hours more light than we did six months ago—for which, many thanks.

Haiku:

> Midsummer
> Rain on the window
> Trees dripping

June 22, 2000; 7:30 a.m.; Grand Beach
My Love,
> Pale blue sky
> Surf foam on the beach
> Solstice days

June 23, 2000; 7:45 a.m.; Grand Beach
My Love,

I read yesterday George Moore's book *The Lake*, about a priest losing his faith. I also read a book by a man who left the Jesuits (before ordination) to become a classics scholar. Both were portraits of a Church that had some impact on my life, kind of a half generation before me. It is a Church that kind of overlapped with mine and influenced me somewhat.

Was I ever blessed to have escaped it! Yet, there were good things in it that have been lost. Thus, the comradeship between the priests in *The Lake* was something that would rarely exist today.

My vocation, it might be said, came out of that era. Or perhaps from the experience that I read in Father Paddy Daly's current book of poems, mediator between You and people. It's still the vocation I ply, in however many different forms.

Who knows what goes into a vocation? Far more complicated than it used to seem. I have no regrets, as You know, save that I am so much a "new" priest in my spirituality. I have not even begun to grow . . . I will continue to try.

I love You.

June 25, 2000; 10:05 a.m.; Grand Beach
My Love,
  Another haiku:

> Dark low clouds
> Above the gray lake
> Thick moist air

June 27, 2000; 8:35 a.m.; Grand Beach
My Love,
  Paddy Daly tells You in his poem this morning that he has been working hard on the task of comforting your people but has found that their pains are so great and his resources so weak that he has come back to tell You to comfort them yourself! Yeah! I know the feeling, but my reflection point today is on the priest's role to comfort. I do a lot of that on e-mail and hopefully through my novels. Yet, what makes it so hard are the idiots, the leaders who want to add yet more burdens to their backs, those blasphemers who think they have a monopoly on You and even make elaborate theological arguments that everyone else has to listen but they don't.

Well, most people don't listen to them anymore, but enough do to suffer because of their words and their deeds. Not much I can do about that, except try.

Why oh why are we so cruel? Who made us, You?
I love You.

July 3, 2000; 8:50 a.m.; Grand Beach
My Love,

I am reading a book by a man who is both a sociologist and an M.D., about prognostication by doctors and how and why they avoid it. He thinks wrongly. I am reminded of Dr. Phee, who never hesitated and, in my case, was always right. I pray for him as his life, filled with so much good, ends in shambles. Take care of him and protect him, I beg You. Also, help me to think about and prepare for my final time in the hospital, whenever in your providence it comes and in whatever way You decide. In the meantime, I thank You for the freedom of our country we celebrate this weekend.

I love You.

July 6, 2000; 7:50 a.m.; Grand Beach
My Love,

The long Fourth of July weekend is over, fogged in three days. Still foggy. You know what I'm like on dark days!

Anyway, today is a quiet day—till supper time, when I must go into Chicago for my flight to Syracuse. Bad idea. I must be delightful. Then back here for guests. Good idea. Then nothing for the rest of the summer.

I must stop running. How often have I told You this? And how often has the world stepped in and demanded that I run? Help me I beg You.

I love You.

July 12, 2000; 9:10 a.m.; Grand Beach
My Love,

My mother's birthday. I'm sure she's happy with You. She was a good woman who had a very hard life. She made it possible for me to have a good life, both by bringing me into the world and by encouraging me in both my education and the priesthood. I thank You for her and I look forward to meeting her again.

I regret that I have not made nearly as much of the spiritual possibilities that You and she have given me. I must continue to try in all the tragedy that might lie ahead.

I love You.

July 13, 2000; 7:25 a.m.; Grand Beach
My Love,

I've been reading about the Korean War, or more specifically, about the Marine retreat from the Chosen Reservoir, where my friend and classmate Curt Kiesling was killed. I bought the book because, in glancing at it in Borders, I saw his name in the index and read an account of his death—a brave volunteer, a quick and trivial death, and a great talent wasted. I have memorialized him as Chris Kurtz in my O'Malley saga. All so long ago: fifty years. We all will pass and be forgotten with the rest, as the song says. I will join him sometime soon. In the World to Come will he know about my books, my dedication of the next one to his memory (in which dedication I promote him from corporal to lieutenant)? Or will it matter? What, indeed, will matter?

And what a terrible thing war is! The battle scenes are dramatic, chilling, and tragic. And all the poor Chinese kids who were slaughtered! My mind shudders at it. Curt's death meant a lot to me. Yet, one of so many! Do You care for them all? Did You wipe away all their tears? Are they safe at home now? I hope so.

How can You love so many people? I believe that You do. Therefore, You love me, though so often I am not very lovable and I have wasted so much in my life.

Of course, I love You. Help me to love You more.

July 14, 2000; 8:10 a.m.; Grand Beach
My Love,

Today I reflect on memory and the purification thereof. I have a powerful and vivid memory—that's why I tell stories, usually without needing to do too much research to tie down events. Also, I try to preserve (as did Proust) things past for those who were not there. Thus, there are not many people who are still alive who would remember Curtis Kiesling. Yet, I want to preserve that era of which he was a part. I want, as it were, to put my spin on the century—as I do also in my memoirs.

My vivid memory—so useful in my work—is also a burden because I remember especially the hurts and the slights of the past as well. At this moment, I think of an especially mean thing that was done to me in August 1947—as clearly as though it happened yesterday. I have no desire to get even with the people who did it, but I remember. I'm thinking of a column on Fatima and talking to a woman outside of church on January 1, 1960. I find myself wondering how I could even talk to her when the pastor didn't want us talking to the laity after Mass.

Silly, silly, silly! Yet, indeed, my memory is disordered and to some extent poisoned. I must strive to become more self-forgetful, to remember and yet not remember, to forget and not forget. I'll need a lot of help to do this.

I love You.

July 15, 2000; 10:30 a.m.; Grand Beach
My Love,

There are three important days in my life: the day I was born (February 5, 1928); the day I was ordained (May 5, 1954); and the day of my death (unknown at this time). The span of my life and the critical event in between. No other dates come to my mind as routinely as do the first two. Birth and priesthood—then the end of life and the end of priesthood, at least the end of the practice of it in this world.

I do not know when the last date will come, when the final bookend will be put in place, when the last chapter will be written. What will I have left behind? I don't know. I can't judge. Anger from lots of people, happiness that I'm gone. Some sorrow from others, intense sorrow from a few. However, those are not the issues. The issue is how I live between now and that fateful day. I must live, not as though I am immortal, but as one who stayed at his lathe until the end, as best he could. So I must try to live, fully aware of my own limitations, but also aware that I must live, not in defiance of those limitations or in defiance of death, but as best I can while the light fades. Help me to do this I beg you.

I love You.

July 16, 2000; 9:00 a.m.; Grand Beach
My Love,

I went waterskiing for the first time this summer and got up just fine—for which, many thanks! I feel great after the exercise. Only problem was climbing back into the boat.

I reflect on control. For seven years at Mundelein and another six years at CK I did not control my life. My appointment to graduate school at the age of thirty-two gave me partial control. Then, when I was released from parish work at the age of thirty-seven, I had complete control (subject to the limitations that come from being human). How happy I was when both those turning points happened. Of course, I did not need to accept the control during by ten years at CK, but I did. Today it would be very different.

Since 1965, I have been master of my own destiny, so to speak. I could do what I wanted, write what I wanted, go where I wanted—more freedom than most people have. My health is still good and that control continues—a great blessing for which I have not been nearly as thankful as I should have been. There are a lot of things I must do (like the wedding at Sagamore last week) because I commit myself to them, but the commitments are my decision—not anyone else's.

The exceptions have been the two times I was in the hospital. I found them irksome, to put it mildly. Others again controlled me. As I face the decline of my physical strength (despite the waterskiing!) and eventual sickness and death, I will have to deal with increased loss of control. I won't like it, but I must be prepared for it and accept it gracefully. By which I mean so that my behavior will be a grace for others. Help me to keep this in mind.

I love You.

July 17, 2000; 8:33 a.m.; Grand Beach
My Love,

I want to reflect on simplicity, a characteristic that does not mark my life in any respect. Quite the contrary; both personally and professionally I am anything but simple. I am a complex, intricate character with many layers of depth wrapped around my inner self, partly at least by design, partly perhaps because I lack most communal and institutional ties. Maybe that latter fact is, in its own way, a form of simplicity. Or maybe it's just that I don't fit.

My lifestyle is not simple. Three homes, each better than the one home most people have. Expensive electronic equipment. Flying around the country and the world. Money spent in improving them all—although each is worth far more now that I have put so much into them.

Yet, am I "attached" to them? Would I find it hard to give up Grand Beach? Will I find it hard when life and death demand that I do? I think, but I'm not sure, that I may weep a little for it, but that I would let go. I hope so.

I've made all the arguments for it before. A place to relax, to work in some kind of peace. I've never been able to solve that problem. Maybe I'm asking the question in the wrong way. I don't know.

Do I need this house on the lake? Perhaps a better question is whether I would have survived without it. I tend to doubt it.

I must reflect more on this simplicity business.

I love You.

July 18, 2000; 9:25 a.m.; Grand Beach
My Love,

The Yoruba prayer I read this morning tells me that You are kind and patient, a God of laughter, and that there is joy in your eye. What a wonderful set of metaphors. I believe them, though perhaps not very strongly. Last night I watched a program about the Battle of Britain. I remember the story, of course, because I was reading the newspapers at the time. However, I was too young to realize the tremendous suffering and tragedy (and how many people believed that England would cave into Hitler). Does a God of joy and laughter tolerate such suffering, which was far worse in many other countries, especially Germany when the English began to bomb back? Moreover, the personal, individual suffering of people who lost their loved ones was incalculable.

I suffered vicariously with them last night and in my dreams and am tormented this morning. They are all elderly now with not much time left. Soon they will join the ones they lost. Soon, I must believe, You will wipe away all tears. Yet, what kind of a parent is it who permits such evil to befall his beloved children? I know that there is no answer to that. And I do believe that You are, among other things, a God of joy and laughter, and that joy and laughter will survive regardless of what happens. Sometimes it's hard, but it's not supposed to be easy.

I love You.

July 19, 2000; 11:00 a.m.; Grand Beach
My Love,

Two Chinese poems this morning. One tells me that as water is to the fish, so Tao (You) is to me. The fish sinks deeply into the water, the human into Tao. True enough, though through my long life (a blessing) I have not done it very well.

Then another poet points out that when an archer is shooting, he is very good, but when he is shooting for the prize, he sees two targets and loses. Or, in more modern terms, Shaq makes all his free throws in practice and usually misses half of them during the game. He should try to concentrate on the shot and forget about the game. As if anyone could. Still, how many times have I experienced that in life. Not very self-forgetful, huh? Though I am, in writing novels. I write the kind of stories I want to write, and I don't worry about any prize. In most other areas, I am too complex to be that self-forgetful.

One of the reasons that my life is not simple is that I must, as a priest, respond to people. That takes a lot of time. No excuse, however. It doesn't take that much time. The problem is not people but memories, angry memories.

An e-mail yesterday attacking me for being a Cubs fan (in response to my column on the difference between Cubs fans and Sox fans) also attacked me for writing dirty novels. Gratuitous nastiness. At least I didn't reply. But if I were deep enough into Tao I would have laughed it off.

Complicated stuff. Haven't figure it out yet. I have a long way to go.

I love You.

July 20, 2000; 10:15 a.m.; Grand Beach
My Love,

Reason is good, the poet tells me this morning. You approve of reason. But reason is not enough, especially it is not enough to account for life or to help us to live the way we should.

I compare that insight with the findings reported on TV last night: that more than three quarters of Americans believe in angels and that three quarters of those who believe feel that they have been touched by an angel. I link this with the Harry Potter phenomenon. Both reveal the human hunger for wonder and surprise, for reassurance that there are realities in charge who take care of us, that You are not distant and disinterested but walking among us like Roma Downey in the TV series. These beliefs, like belief in heaven and life after death, would cause most scientists and academics and other members of the cultural elite to raise their eyebrows in dismay at the persistence of superstition.

Are there really entities that have direct charge of us in addition to your overarching care for us? I hope so. I don't think angels are a matter of faith. In the Jewish scriptures, they represent You dealing with humans. Yet, I would like to think that there are benign beings in the cosmos who look after us in your name, not because You can't do it all yourself, but because it pleases You to work that way. In any case, we are protected under the shadow of your wing, despite all the bad things that happen to good people. Ultimately, neither You nor your angels are wish-fulfillment.

I love You.

July 21, 2000; 8:40 a.m.; Grand Beach
My Love,

The poet, a certain Wang Wei, tells me this morning that no one will ask about me when I'm gone. He adds, however, that there are white clouds in the mountains (and, I would note, also over the lake). It applies. I have worked very, very hard and produced an extensive bibliography of stuff, most of which is ignored now and was ignored when it appeared. What people say about me is not who I am. And I'm tired. *Cui bono,* as we used to say. When I'm gone, I'm nothing at all—or practically nothing. That's overstated perhaps. The point is that one does not achieve immortality through one's work but only through one's love. Not that I wrote all I have to achieve fame or immortality. Those concerns have always been irrelevant. I wanted only that people would listen. Mostly they did not. Even that is not so important. I would write if only a few people would listen. Still, just now, on this lovely morning, I understand Aquinas—*mihi videtur ut pavia.* Dust!

I cannot and should not stop, not now. But I should grow more detached from it; teach us to care and not to care, huh?

I love You.

July 22, 2000; 9:47 a.m.; Grand Beach
My Love,

So many wonders in the world. Take for example the exhilaration of skiing today, or the breathtaking loveliness of my garden. When I water-ski, I feel better all day long. How marvelous that the human organism is built for exercising, and is so stimulated by it.

Or the garden, particularly the various blue flowers. How wonderful that the world needs various colored flowers to keep the food chains in harmony.

I can't ignore the wonder of skiing because it physically possesses me, although I am not grateful enough for it. I can ignore the beauty of the garden as it flourishes and grows, and for that I am sorry. I'll try to pay more attention to it. I must try to write a poem about it.

I love You.

July 23, 2000; 8:00 a.m.; Grand Beach
My Love,

I note that many flowers in my garden open to greet the sunlight and then close when the sun slips away. You are, according to Brother Wayne, infinite openness. I must strive to be open to You, as the flowers are to the sun. Not easy. Especially when I have skied two days in a row and am as sleepy as I am now, especially since I didn't sleep last night. And if I am open to You, then I will be open to others. Help me to be open and understanding no matter who the other is. So hard.

Also, in Rexroth's poem this morning, the world and its people are described as infinitely small and infinitely large. To care and not to care. There is so much and so many to care about, more than I can absorb. Help me to understand better these paradoxes.

I love You.

July 24, 2000; 10:20 a.m.; Grand Beach
My Love,

The night before last I woke up and believed in nothing. It was a bad night, and I'm not sure why—and I didn't get much sleep. So all the demons, such as these may be, came out. Finally I went back to sleep and, when I woke up, my faith had returned. It was a kind of waking nightmare, with chaos swirling around me and darkness closing in on all sides. And it was cold. Or was it hot? I don't remember.

If, as the storyteller said, the line between love and hate is as thin as a razor's edge, so is the line between belief and unbelief. If we are honest, we admit that we skate all life long close to the edge of that line—or should I say chasm.

The poet this morning, an anonymous Bushman, says that when we die, the wind blows away our footprints. A nice way of putting it! Footprints don't have much substance, do they. Does anything remain after the footprints? In the dark of night, that seemed unlikely. Now, in the light of day, I believe that something does, regardless of my fears in the dark of night. Yet, I do not kid myself that faith is easy. Rather, it is always clinging with my fingertips to the hints of love that are always around in the daylight hours. Yet, there is so much goodness, so much beauty, so much love!

I love You.

July 26, 2000; 8:40 a.m.; Grand Beach

My Love,

I read a chapter from Jose Hobday this morning and discovered this wonderful prayer of the Three Steps:

> O Great God (or Great Spirit, if you want to use Native American language), you give me this day as a special gift. In taking this step into the day, I accept everything it will bring, whether part of my plan or not. Teach me to accept every gift that comes my way today. Help me to use each gift wisely, to love my brothers and sisters, and to care for my Mother the Earth.
>
> O Great God (or Great Spirit), you created me as I am. In taking this step, I accept myself as a I am, as I have been in the past, and as I will be in the future. I ask that today I will be true to the way you made me. Help me to walk respectfully on my Mother the Earth so none of its plants will be crushed. Help me to walk into people's lives in the same way, so none will be bruised.
>
> O Great God (or Great Spirit), you created me and everything around me with a sense of mystery. I now step into that mystery and put my arms around it. Help me to accept the things of this day I do not and cannot understand. Help me to use the encounters with mystery to draw nearer to you, to my brothers and sisters, and to all you have made.

It's essentially a prayer of acceptance and it tells me how to accept each day with both its joys and frustrations and its sense of eroding summer and eroding life. I'm going to try to say it every morning. Thank You for the impulse to pick up her book.

I love You.

July 27, 2000; 7:35 a.m.; Grand Beach

My Love,

My efforts at contemplation this morning were once again severely distracted. I live in an environment were distractions are endemic. The phone was silent. There were no faxes. The house was quiet. I made a good start. Then the world broke through. 'Tis ever thus, isn't it? My mind and my imagination are so agile that they are almost always out of control. I don't know what to do about it. I know You love me, even as I am distracted. I know You want me to keep trying. I also know You want me to figure out a way, after all these years, to do it better. I keep thinking that I have to find the right time and the right place. But I've never found it. After lunch, when I've cleared away the morning work, is probably the best time. I will try tomorrow and through the weekend and not put it off till the end of the day.

Today I read about presence and listening, and I worry about my e-mail parish. I wonder if I am too hasty in dealing with them. They have become a terrible burden. Perhaps I dismiss them too briefly, too quickly. There are so many different varieties of people with different needs. I could spend all day on them, but that's not what You want. Anyway, I must be more aware of my propensity to dismiss people who need help because they take so much of my time. In some cases, a line or two is appropriate. In other cases, I should be more thoughtful.

I love You.

July 28, 2000; 10:55 a.m.; Grand Beach
My Love,

Jose tells me today that the Native Americans have four days for Thanksgiving and express gratitude to eighteen realities before they get to You. I bet You just love that! Like an artist dotes on praise for his paintings and an author on praise for his book (this author included), so You dote on praise and gratitude for the splendors of your creation! The place I'm in is surely one of the most beautiful in the world. Beats the Vineyard and the Hamptons and the Adirondacks—all hollow. Costa Brava and Amalfi are good but inadequate rivals. I love its beauty and enjoy it often, perhaps not often enough. I must try to thank You constantly, every day, for this beauty.

I love You.

July 29, 2000; 6:10 a.m.; Grand Beach
My Love,

Of the many weaknesses in my spirituality is my lack of attention to and faith in my experience that You are a vulnerable lover who seeks a response, not because You need it but because You want it. The problem, as always, is that it is very hard to picture the One who started the Big Bang and presides over the immense number of rapidly moving galaxies as being concerned about us tiny and insignificant creatures. Indeed, sometimes the tragedies in life seem to be evidence of your lack of concern. Yet, I do believe that You care about each of us as a parent cares about children. The alternative to that is madness.

Science thinks that, for example, when it explains the beauty of the flowers in my garden, it has explained everything. But for all its explanations it cannot cope with the Great Mystery of why there is anything at all, including the beauty of the flowers. It seems to me that the one who is behind the beauty of the flowers, however indirectly, must care. But I don't act like that often, do I? And I'm so sleepy at this hour of the morning, it's hard to care about anything except going back to bed! What a weak and imperfect being

I am. Still, I know You love me.
And I try to love You.

July 31, 2000; 7:35 a.m.; Grand Beach
My Love,

Last day of July—halfway through the summer, though my summer still has six weeks to go. Terrible day again: rain, fog, dark. So I'm caught in gloom. Nonetheless, I am grateful for July and its blessings. I am somewhat relaxed and refreshed. There is a certain beauty in the weather. Everything is as green as it was in June. My lawn is pure emerald. The garden is soggy but also very green. When the sun comes out, nature will run wild again, just as it does in spring. A second spring! If the sun returns tomorrow and the world begins to dry out, it will be a kind of revelation too. The world drying out is especially attractive.

No poetry yet this summer. But I'm going to try this week.
I love You.

August 1, 2000; 8:10 a.m.; Grand Beach
My Love,

I assume, for the sake of today's argument, that You love everyone with the tender love of a parent. I don't know how that's possible, but I'm not supposed to know how that's possible, right? I also assume that somehow You are vulnerable as You present yourself in the Jewish scriptures. Again, I don't understand how You can be, but the suffering of Jesus assures me that You are. Therefore, in some fashion, You suffer when we do—when the baby weeps, God cries. Again, I don't know how this can be true, but I know that it is true.

Having thus fought my way through the thickets of three dense mysteries, I ask myself, how much do You suffer each of our days when so many of your children are starved, tortured, raped, and murdered. It must come close to overwhelming You. I know You can't be overwhelmed, but if You are burdened with all the suffering in the world—not a sparrow falls—it must be, how should I say it, a daunting experience. Even if You can't be daunted.

Moreover, like every lover, You want to be loved. Yet, how many of us ignore You, myself included. We don't believe that You really need us, so we go through our days and nights paying little or no attention to You. What idiots!

I must keep telling myself over and over again that You want to hear that I love You.

So I end, as I always do—and today with a deeper sense of the necessity of saying it:
I love You!

August 2, 2000; 8:40 a.m.; Grand Beach
My Love,

You are like the sun breaking through the fog! Not a very original metaphor, I admit. But the sun did break through the fog and illumine everything for a few moments and then went away again. Fog in August!

Anyway, we can explain fog and we can explain that the sun is merely a small star in a small galaxy. We know that neither it nor we are all that important and probably not unique. Yet, the sun bursting through the fog is nonetheless dramatic—spectacular beauty despite all our science, which has lost its sense of wonder and surprise. It loses none of its beauty because we can put it in its place. (Please send the sun back again; it is as elusive these days as You are!) And You came to be for a few moments in my contemplation this morning, breaking through, as always, on your own terms, despite my distractions. It was nice to be with You again. It's so hard for me to accept that You are aware enough of me to notice that I am trying to open myself to You and to respond to my poor efforts at love.

But I believe that You are, indeed, and that I should try to stay in touch with You throughout the day.

I love You. Help me to say it over and over again.

August 3, 2000; 8:00 a.m.; Grand Beach
My Love,

I'm reading Father Paddy Daly's poems. The one this morning depicts morning at an English public-housing site with the doors to the houses opening and people emerging into the cold winter air (not cold by our standards, of course). He says that if You are anywhere, You are there.

Indeed, yes! Surely You are present in the flowers in my garden, in the clear blue sky, in the turbulent lake, in the refreshing northeast wind. You are also present in the men and women going to work, kids going to school—in the awakening day of ordinary people . . . in the crowds that will swarm around my house this weekend. Help me to be aware of your presence in all of them.

Help me, too, to stay in touch with You in the course of this day, to represent You and your love to everyone I see.

I love You.

August 4, 2000; 8:55 a.m.; Grand Beach
My Love,

I've been collecting metaphors for You:

You're the sun breaking through a dense fog.
You're the northeast wind seeping away humidity.
You're a peaceful dusk after a terrible day.

You're the reassuring sound of the surf during a restless night.
You are a clean and empty beach in very early morning.

Paddy Daly, in his poem this morning, compares You to the smells of a farm, unbearably sweet and close. I don't know from farms. I do know from this place. I must try more to be aware of You wherever I am—and thus grow to love You more than I do.
I love You.

August 8, 2000; 9:15 a.m.; Grand Beach
My Love,

In Paddy Daly's poems this morning, he depicts You hovering over everyone and whispering in their ears at night, "the surfeited and starved, the whole, the hurt, the broken-hearted." He then says that when affection swamps him, he trusts that You can cope with the "overwhelming sea."

Do I know that feeling! There's so many people I would like to help! Even those I saw in the ice cream parlor last night. It is as though the whole world is my mission field. Long ago I gave up hope of helping everyone—which was a presumptuous notion anyway. Now I wonder if it is possible to help anyone. I try.

Do You have similar feelings? Or should I say analogous ones? Do we overwhelm even You with our needs? Should we wonder about helping You? I know You don't need our help, but I suspect that You would be pleased if we asked. Like I say, I try. Not very effectively—but I try. My novels are the strongest of my efforts. Sometimes with some people they work. Thank You for that grace.
I love You.

August 11, 2000; 9:05 a.m.; Grand Beach
My Love,

This morning I observe that being assumed into heaven might be a good idea for everyone. I find that it is not death that troubles me, but the aging and sickness and failure of body and soul that precedes death that is obnoxious. Three of my friends are sick in one way or another, two will not recover. One I hope will. Only to eventually die, as we all must.

If I may say so, with all due respect, it's not fair that You could create beings that are conscious of their own mortality and at the same time hunger for immortality. Father Daly this morning cries out about his frustrations that he cannot adequately respond to those who have lost people they love to tragedy. I know the feeling, if I may say so. Perhaps, as I said to Bob Barron this week, this is not the best possible universe at all, but the one that this particular Big Bang happened to produce. Maybe You did better in other big bangs. But what do I know!

I have been asked three times this week why my energy and enthusiasm continue to flourish and why my storytelling gets better. The answer? Lucky genes, I guess. Or, to give the phenomenon another name, grace—for which, many thanks. We work while the light lasts.

And, despite my complaints, I love You.

August 13, 2000; 7:55 a.m.; Grand Beach
My Love,

I come upon Paddy Daly's great poem in which You are compared to a mother cleaning out the house in preparation for her children's return home (from school perhaps). It moved me deeply the first time I read it. It still moves me. Are You really that way, I wonder. Do You care for each of us with such poignant attention to detail? Do You hold each of us in the palm of your hand? If You really do, then there is nothing to fear. There may be pain and suffering, but it will be all right in the end. The tragedy of life will be cancelled out by love, the deterioration will be reserved. We will go home to peace and happiness, whatever that will mean.

Summer slips away, as it always does. I must strive to devote more time to You because You devote so much time to me—even if time is not something You experience. At least that's what the philosophers and the theologians say. But what do they know?

I love You.

August 14, 2000; 7:00 a.m.; Grand Beach
My Love,

Father Daly writes this morning about an aunt and uncle who seemed to have missed out on life. How fragile happiness is, he tells us. I think of my own uncles and aunts who had such difficult lives and so little happiness. I think of my cousins, most of whom I haven't seen in years. Some have had plenty of happiness, thanks be to You. Only one is special to me and I never see her because she lives far away. A woman of great courage and stubborn joy. There is a nod to her in one of my characters. For a time, I tried to keep up with them, but then my first years in the priesthood, six of them without a car, made it impossible. Then I went off in other directions. To generalize, many people mostly suffer in life, some most of the time. I feel that I should do something for them. But what can I do? I can at least pray for them, but that seems so inadequate. Still, I beg You to take care of them—and I know that You will.

I love You.

August 15, 2000; 8:20 a.m.; Grand Beach
My Love,

Paddy Daly's poems this morning make me feel melancholy. He laments for all the lost opportunities in life, opportunities that perhaps had to be lost, but not all. How very Irish. I know the feeling from the inside. I, too, lament for all I might have done, much of which is my own fault. I have had, for a long time, a sense of waste in my life. That sounds crazy from someone who has done so much. But . . . but I have let love slip through my fingers. Or maybe I haven't. Maybe on balance I've done all I can. I don't know.

Yet, the voice within keeps coming back. It keeps saying that I have failed to respond to grace, I have missed opportunities, I have wasted so much. In my defense (against myself, perhaps against You, though I'm not sure), I say that I've tried and that now I'm tired and lament the end of summer on this Lady Day in Harvest Time. I will keep trying, but there is so much to do. Need I, for example, be so alienated from the archdiocese? I supposed I do.

In this interlude of feeling worthless, I renew my love for You and beg You to help me be responsive to You on this harvest festival. I regret the lost opportunities.

I love You.

August 16, 2000; 9:45 a.m.; Grand Beach
My Love,

Father Daly says today that when I reach out to You, I have already found You; that when I move my hand, You are there. When I sit at the keyboard to do these meditations—to adapt his metaphor a bit—You are already with me, wanting me, loving me, caring for me (Lonergan and Tracy with a vengeance)! I believe that. But I don't always live that way, do I? Moreover, I am not nearly as conscious of your presence as I want to be. Help me—especially on days like this.

I love You.

August 18, 2000; 8:30 a.m.; Grand Beach
My Love,

I've been watching a British TV series about the Eighth Air Force in Britain in 1943 and the interaction of the airmen with the local English townsfolk. It borders on soap opera, but the historical details are generally accurate, and it revives in my mind the memories of that era—one, of course, reflected in novels and films (*12 O'Clock High*) about that situation. I am impressed by the risks, the bravery, the tragedy of that time—brave Germans too. Life was so short for so many of the men. And the strategic bombing survey after the war demonstrated that it was a waste.

Those that lived are now in their late seventies, although they were only a few years older—maybe five—than I was at that time. Those that lived through the mess are now either dead or close to death. May You grant them all rest and peace.

I conclude that death comes anyway and that I must accept that fact while, at the same time, living like one who is not greatly worried about death because he trusts in your love. I tend to get morose about it at times and fail to catch myself, especially up here where there is so much beauty that I can easily lament the loss. Will I be back here next year? I don't know. It's all up to You, but I must live like I will, but be ready to accept whatever might come before that.

I love You.

August 20, 2000; 6:55 a.m.; Grand Beach

My Love,

Father Daly has a sad line in his poem today: "Long ago when there was hope/before life cankered us." I had that experience these last couple of days when I read volume 3 of the *History of the Second Vatican Council.* So much excitement, so much hope, so much conspiracy, so much corruption. Now the hope is virtually gone, the energies of the council dissipated, the old guard back in power, the credibility of the Church and of the papacy sadly diminished. We won but we lost. We all lost. We keep on losing.

Then there was a time when I thought I could be the sociologist for the archdiocese. Not once in the forty years since I began to study.

So many other sad stories.

Yet, while many hopes have been cankered, I still am a man of hope, because of your grace. I work and write because I still hope, though my expectations are not all that great. Grant that I may continue to try.

I love You.

August 21, 2000; 8:25 a.m.; Grand Beach

My Love,

Father Daly tells this morning how even the most beautiful things do not always confirm faith. Indeed, our emptiness sometimes grows worse when a reality that is strikingly beautiful leaves us dull and bleak. But then, at the right time, something very minor opens us up to You.

The trick, I think, is to be open always to your presence. Then one won't miss the presence of grace when tears open the reality of life and permit You to rush in. Like the furrows on the surface of the lake this morning.

I love You.

August 23, 2000; 8:55 a.m.; Grand Beach

My Love,

Priests this week. Good priests—hardworking, creative, inspiring. Also worn out and discouraged. I was discouraged, too. So many things going wrong, mostly because insensitive and arrogant leadership and lazy mediocre priests. Terrible, terrible crisis. All the energies of the Council dissipated and almost destroyed. The reform has just begun. It is our fate to live in the time when the new Church is struggling to be born. Very difficult. "What happens when we die?" they asked several times. "Who will replace us?" Fair question because there is no one in sight to replace them. I quoted the famous John Quinn story—"Too bad for God! It's his fault!"

The point of the story is that You permitted the present mess for reasons of your own, and that when we die, it's up to You, not us, what comes next. Which gives You a heavy responsibility, I guess. Presumably, You can cope with it.

All kidding aside, please help us!

I love You.

August 24, 2000; 12:05 p.m.; Grand Beach

My Love,

Busy morning. Only get to this reflection at noon, after having tried for four hours. Last night one of my priest guests said a nice thing about hearing the lake thump against the beach: that after a while it does the work! I haven't given it much of a chance to do that this summer, but I must seize the opportunities still left and give myself over to listening to the lake. This morning, while I was doing it, the phone rang for a twenty-minute necessary conversation!

Well, such is the nature of the human condition, at least as I live it.

I am being stalked by a crazy woman who wants to have "Communion" with me! I have ignored her e-mails, but that didn't stop her from showing up at my door with sweet rolls, bread, and wine! I've warned her off. She does not seem physically dangerous, but who knows? Protect me, please. I don't want to be cruel, but I don't think I have any choice.

A strange world You have created!

Help me to love You more and let the lake do the work.

August 25, 2000; 8:45 a.m.; Grand Beach

My Love,

Father Paddy's poem this morning is about the gift of a blanket for which he is grateful. He compares it to your protective blanket over all of us.

You are actually concerned about protecting me? Keeping me warm? This is hard to comprehend, almost impossible. Yet, I believe it to be true. And in that belief, however weak and uncertain, I find comfort and confidence. Every day is precious now.

I love You.

August 28, 2000; 7:45 a.m.; Grand Beach

My Love,

Father Daly today pictures You as a noble returning from a hunt, with a hound in front of You to protect You from humans! Wow! What an image! Another metaphor for the Hidden God, the Absconded God.

I have no problems with You absconding. That's your business. I know that You are still around. My problems are with figuring out who You are and how You are consistent with things like food chains. And tragedy. All life is tragic. I can't believe You like unhappy endings . . . So tragedy doesn't have the last word.

I love You.

August 29, 2000; 8:05 a.m. Grand Beach

My Love,

This morning I don't seem to care about a lot of things, probably because I didn't sleep all that well last night. And the reason for that is I worked straight through until 11:00 last night—which is crazy.

The summer is slipping away. Once more I regret the waste of it. I'm sorry. I don't look forward to the coming year. Too much. I must cut back. Help me.

I love You.

August 30, 2000, 8:30 a.m.; Grand Beach

My Love,

I watched *La Traviata* on TV last night—in places in Paris where it might actually have happened. Has there ever been a greater opera? Or a more Catholic one?

I'm not even typing right this morning!

Violeta is clearly a Christ figure. Did Verdi realize that? I'm sure he didn't. But his Catholic imagination, filled with images of sacrificial love and salvation, saw the story where someone else surely would not have.

And what about the real Lady of the Camellias? Did she obtain salvation, poor kid?

Surely she did because You are a God of mercy and love, nothing but mercy and love.

And I love You.

August 31, 2000; 10:50 a.m.; Grand Beach
My Love,

August over soon—soon! Not fair.

Still, thank You for all the graces You have bestowed on me this summer. Despite my sleep deprivation routine yesterday, I am quite relaxed, though bitterly opposed to returning to the city—which I will do grudgingly and ungraciously!

Last night the sun set in a thick haze and looked like a red beach ball that someone had bounced into the air. It hung in the sky like it would quickly fall back to the beach. I had the thought that it was, after all, your beach ball, and You might get tired of bouncing it! Obviously it is not a beach ball—and just as obviously You don't play games with your stars, even ones that are arguably quite unimportant. Your Big Bang is a much more spectacular game, even if it is hard to understand—and even harder to understand why. Why things like food chains, for example? Yet, I look at the gorgeous purple flowers in my garden—I really should learn their names, shouldn't I? You are as much behind them as You are behind the sun and the Big Bang. You support all beings in their being, which is very clever of You, is it not? Why do You do that? I guess because You want to.

Impressive. But odd . . .

I went into New Buffalo this morning for a haircut—an annual summer event, whether I need it or not. Although today will be the hottest day of the summer—up in the mid-nineties—there was a pleasant early morning breeze in the air. Also a clever trick.

As You can see, I'm in one of my odd moods.

But still I love You very much.

September 1, 2000, 8:10 a.m.; Grand Beach
My Love,

August over. Only two weeks left up here. A lot to do.

I'm very sleepy this morning, but I still love You. I'm sure You love me too, even when I'm sleepy. Perhaps especially when I'm sleepy because then I'm willing to leave a lot more to You.

I love You.

September 2, 2000; 6:50 a.m.; Grand Beach
My Love,

I'm up early to go skiing. Not much sleep either. Bad start.

As I mourn the end of summer, I tell myself that very few people have a chance for a summer like mine—the lake, this house, my friends up here, leisure, good health (despite my occasional hypochondria), and confidence in your love. The latter was reinforced yesterday by finishing Robert Wright's

Nonzero. I think he's pretty much correct about what You're up to in creation, and that consciousness, if it isn't *Le Point Omega*, is pretty close to it. Evolution, biological and cultural, is an incredible phenomenon. Very clever of You. So I add time to read to the list of undeserved blessings.

For these and all other gifts, I'm deeply grateful.

And I love You.

September 3, 2000; 8:10 a.m.; Grand Beach

My Love,

I failed again at waterskiing this morning. Sean says it's because I'm not ready, not hunched properly over the skis. I think he's right. Should I try again tomorrow or give it up till next year? When I'll be seventy-three!

Maybe it is time to be sensible.

I find myself wondering whether I should be doing more priestly work during the summer. Perhaps it isn't priestly enough just to write columns and homilies for the web, to do sociology, and to write novels—and sit down on the deck reading.

Put that way, the question is silly. Each one must work his own lathe, must follow the Spirit's prompting. Long ago I decided that stepping aside from the chaos in summer was appropriate and virtuous. It still is, I think. But who knows? You do, of course. I hope You understand and approve, but I can't be certain. I know that, regardless, You still love me.

As I try to love You.

September 4, 2000 (Labor Day); 7:50 a.m.; Grand Beach

My Love,

The formal end of summer. The weather cooperates—gray, cool, windy, big waves, and gloomy. Matches my spirit, alas.

Still, once again, thank You for all the gifts and blessings of the summer. Help me to keep my head during the tasks and tensions of the autumn. As I have said, I have ten different projects to keep alive through the fall, more work on one of them just came through this morning. I'm not going to work on it today, though, for which I think I deserve great credit!

I feel both lonely and alone today, rare feelings for me. I have that sense again that I've frittered away my time and energy on stupid things. Perhaps I have. Perhaps I could have done better. But at least I take consolation in the thought that You love me, despite all my inadequacies and failures.

And I try to love You.

September 5, 2000; 8:20 a.m.; Grand Beach

My Love,

Now begins, for all practical purposes, autumn. The cold weather this morning feels like autumn. However, my work cycle changes. I don't merely do a little bit of work all day. Now I work all day. I look forward to my work and dread it at the same time. At least, and this is a great blessing, it is almost always interesting. I don't like to begin it, but when I have done so, I enjoy the exercise of creating stories or understanding social reality better. I must try to do it and not become compulsive, not wear myself out emotionally and spiritually while I work. To be dragged out at the end of the day is not to be in tune with the reality of the world around me.

Which brings me to the second part of my reflection this morning. I am so dull and insensitive spiritually. I love the beauty of the world around me, but I am not very skilled in bringing that reality inside myself in my contemplation. I must try to do that more during my remaining two weeks up here before I return to the maelstrom of Chicago.

The top of the tree swaying in the brisk wind is an image I must keep in my head all day. For You are in both the tree and the wind.

I love You, despite my spiritual dullness.

September 6, 2000; 8:40 a.m.; Grand Beach
My Love,

Yesterday I saw You in the top of the tree waving in the breeze. Today Brother Wayne talks about the Spirit in creation. And the tree trimming companies are clearing out my dune. I feel kind of guilty. The lake, however, has a spirit too, and I should be able to see it. Thinning out trees is sometimes necessary. I still feel kind of guilty.

I wondered last night as I tried to go to sleep why I am an outcast almost everywhere—in the archdiocese, at the university, with my old group of friends, in the literary world. What is it in my character that causes these problems? Perhaps it is my combination of roles. Perhaps it is my propensity to take on odd causes. Perhaps I speak my mind too much. Perhaps I am, as someone remarked years ago, a loudmouth Irish priest. Which is surely true.

(I was afraid that a worker was about to take out a tree I wanted to save. He didn't!)

It is probably too late in life to change. And probably I shouldn't change even if I could. I'm a marginal man, partly by necessity and partly by choice, but it does give me freedom.

What do I know? Maybe I've made a lot of mistakes. No, I *have* made a lot of mistakes. I'm sorry about them.

I know You still love me, regardless. I try to love You.

September 7, 2000; 8:50 a.m.; Grand Beach
My Love,

Brother Wayne has a wonderful story about how he reassured a frightened falcon that had fallen off a ledge in Hyde Park. (Why a falcon would have chosen to live in that ugly neighborhood is another matter!) It's a lovely story about a man's ability to break across the species barrier and commune with nature (and I don't doubt its truth for a moment). It makes me realize that, despite my love of nature and its beauty and my writing about sacramentality in nature, I have very little sensitivity to your presence in nature. What a terribly dull and prosaic man I am!

The people next door are doing their tree trimming the day after I did (by chance). They are tearing down a lot of trees, including the one I imagined You at the top of a few days ago. Because of Brother Wayne, I am sad about this—though, as I said yesterday, a case can be made for freeing the view of the lake. I would be more reassured by that case if I thought I was sensitive to the lake, as much as I like it.

I rush through life too quickly. I still am rushing at this moment—and I'm sorry about that.

I love You.

September 8, 2000; 8:05 a.m.; Grand Beach
My Love,

Little sleep last night after a horrendous day. Phones, phones, phones!

Someone asked me the other night what I would be if I had not become a priest. Good question! I was so single-minded in my determination to become a priest that I didn't think of anything else. Odd, wasn't it? Moreover, if I had left the priesthood—and, as You know, the idea never occurred to me—I would have had a couple of occupations that would have lost most of their attraction if I were not a priest.

Is this single-mindedness a good thing? I guess I really don't know for sure. It can't be said that I ever seriously considered marriage either. I was infatuated a couple of times but from a great distance and never seriously.

One track mind. Healthy? I don't know. That's what I am, however. Dedicated—or maybe only stubborn.

No regrets surely, none at all. As life winds down, I'm as certain as ever. I would, as the man said in the book, "do it all again!"

Would I have been better off—and maybe a better priest—if I had gone through some other considerations? Maybe. Who knows? I am what I am.

And I love You.

September 11, 2000; 7:55 a.m.; Grand Beach
My Love,

The trip to Chicago on Saturday wiped me out. I get too tired too easily. I suspect the strain of my tedious work last week had caught up with me. I was tense and angry much of the time. Of course I held it back, which was the right thing to do.

George Coyne's talk, however, was wonderful. We are all, he said, stardust—which is a wonderful thought. A hundred billion stars in our galaxy and a hundred billion galaxies. Excessive! Why so much?

I am forced back to my argument that You were showing off. For which I don't blame You. If I were God, I would show off too!

I'm still suffering from sleep deprivation, and I'm a little uneasy that I'm exhausted at the end of summer, when I should be refreshed. For the rest of this week, I will stop working at noon. Maybe write a poem or two. Try to recollect.

Sorry to let myself get so worn out.

I love You.

September 12, 2000; 9:00 a.m.; Grand Beach
My Love,

I stood on the dune yesterday afternoon and watched the storm come down the lake, headed right at me, or so it seemed. When I was a kid, scared by the apocalyptic gospels, I would ask whether it might be the end of the world. It was an end-of-the-world storm: fifty-mile-an-hour winds; low, dark, dark clouds; a green lake with huge whitecaps; trees bending over like they were going to break; fierce rain beating against the windows when I ducked into the house. Scary, but also beautiful! Then it cleared away and I was able to swim around 10:00 until the lightning came close and the clouds rolled back. The radar screen on the web shows the rain having passed by us, but the storm—or yet another storm—is still howling. O'Hare was closed down much of the day.

Winter, not autumn, is closing in. Fearsome. And also, as I say, beautiful.

The storms show the power of the Lord, as the Scripture says. Even now, when we know that there is far more power in the cosmos and that our earth storms are pretty puny, they'll do as a hint of what You are capable.

I'm relieved on a morning like this to know that You love me.

I try to love You in response.

September 13, 2000; 8:13 a.m.; Grand Beach
My Love,

I've been combing through my limited collection of baby pictures to send to June for the profile PBS is doing. They made me feel very sad. I look at that innocent and happy little boy and feel sorry for him. He did not know the disillusion and the disappointment he was to suffer. He thought every-one loved him because his parents did. He had yet to discover that many people would not love him because he was different and, as it seemed to them, "too much." He wrote too much, he knew too much, he said too much, and he had too much energy and enthusiasm. I wish he could have been preserved from all these things, but there was never a chance.

I remember the body blows to my selfhood each time I encountered this hatred. I'm used to it now, more or less. I understand that I must be an inkblot, a scapegoat. It was your destiny for me. But I still feel sad about it. I'm glad the little boy didn't know. He might have quit.

Anyway, I'm not a scapegoat for You. You love me regardless.

And I try to love You.

September 17, 2000; 8:00 a.m.; Chicago

My Love,

Back in Chicago. The wind against the windows last night reminded me of the waves at the lake. The city is beautiful, though there's an ugly blue sign on a nearby building that ought to be blown up.

Thank You again for the summer. Sorry I wasted so much of it.

On this day in 1947 my father died—fifty-three years ago. He was only sixty, twelve years younger than I am now. Too much smoking, too much stress, too much heartache perhaps.

He had an enormous impact on me, made me a man of principles and integrity. I'm sorry he suffered so much during the Depression, and that we never became really close. On the other hand, I am very grateful that I had such a man as my father, and for that many, many thanks.

We will meet again, in the not-too-distant future, as time goes. I will be interested to get to know him again. I look forward to it. In your good time!

I love him and I love You!

September 19, 2000; 8:25 a.m.; Chicago

My Love,

I have been working very hard the last couple of days, especially on the Irish study, which just drags on. It continues to be very interesting, if terribly difficult because of the mistakes of the data collectors. I wore myself out last night by working till 10:00, against all my rules, and hence slept badly. I'm sorry.

I've been asked how I like being back in Chicago. My answer is that I haven't noticed much because I'm too busy working. No different from Grand Beach.

Why work so hard?

I don't know.

I think this Irish report is very important, not only for Ireland but for the Church and for sociology . . . as is the book I'm working on. I have to do both projects, and I'll be very glad when they're over.

I love You.

September 21, 2000; 8:15 a.m.; Chicago

My Love,

Busy day yesterday. Sorry I had no time. I simply had to clean things off my desk, not that it's ever really cleaned off!

I've been reading about René Girard's work. At first I was skeptical until I realized I was a scapegoat. Interesting experience. Your Son Jesus had it, too. There is a terrible feeling of betrayal. It eases when you understand the mechanism. I now must pray that they do too, though it is not likely they will while I'm still alive.

Come to think of it, I guess I have been a scapegoat several times.

I don't celebrate that, You understand, but it explains a lot of things!

I can at least be easy about it in the sense that I don't have to worry about what I did wrong. We scapegoats must band together!

I love You.

September 23, 2000; 8:35 a.m.; Chicago

My Love,

I did some very stupid things yesterday. After the talk at Rosemont (which went all right, I guess), I was exhausted and came back to the apartment. However, the cleaning person was here, so I set to work on stuff piled in from various places. I worked hard, stopped at 7:00. The swimming pool was locked, so no exercise and relaxation.

Then I had a terrible dream. I was living in the house on Mayfield, and there was an infestation of animals. For some reason I actually brought in elephants. They disappeared early in the story, though. There were also barking puppies. And camels who were destroying the shrubbery. And a tiger with her kittens. The tiger bit off the head of a dog who was harassing her (no blood!). There were also a couple of wandering platypuses. And in the house there was a very pregnant lion who was busy delivering her offspring. I tried desperately to call someone to help, but I couldn't make the phone work (portable phone which, of course, didn't exist on Mayfield Avenue), most because I was not dialing the buttons.

Terrible nightmare of struggle. I woke up exhausted. Couldn't go back to sleep for a couple of hours. Obvious what it was about.

I resolved to slow down, however. This time I really will.

Help me!

I love You.

September 26, 2000; 7:15 a.m.; Chicago
My Love,

I wake up this morning rested, tranquil, relaxed. Alas, it is not because my character or personality have changed, but because I took cough medicine before I went to bed. It dries out my sinus, calms my nerves, cools me down. I take it only when the cough (induced by allergies) won't let me sleep. However, the way I feel this morning is the way I should always feel. Kind of late in life to decide that, isn't it?

A prayer I read this morning suggests that everything happens for the best. I don't believe that. Neither, I think, do You. You can, indeed, convert evil to good, just as You convert helium into hydrogen. But it isn't easy, and You don't approve of a lot of things that happen. That I become a scapegoat and an outcast is not a good thing, but You turn it into good.

That is small stuff. The Holocaust and the Famine were not good things either. The prayer is pangloss. Evil happens. We must learn to resist it as best we can, like the people in Yugoslavia are resisting it today. Help them in their fight for freedom, and help me to realize how precious our freedom is.

I love You.

September 27, 2000; 7:50 a.m.; Chicago
My Love,

Why am I living this way? 7:45 and I'm already at the computer to work on my book on Europe. It is, as I have told You, terribly tedious work, made even more so by phone interruptions. Does the book have to be done? No! Do *I* have to do it? No! Why am I doing it? Because it is *important* and because I *can* do it. Will it have the impact I want it to have? No!

Yet, I continue to wear myself out each day working on it. Why? To get it out of the way so I can go on to other things!

Crazy? I guess so, yet I can't help but feel that it should be done, and You are not displeased with me for working so hard. It's part of the good fight.

I love You.

September 28, 2000; 7:50 a.m.; Chicago
My Love,

Another lovely day in Chicago—and I'm going to spend it at this machine instead of going out for a walk in the early (too early!) Indian summer weather. I should be ashamed of myself.

If You exist, and if there is a reward for being true to one's vocation, the work I'm doing now is worth it. Maybe it will make a dent. I hope so.

If You do not exist (for the sake of an argument), I'm wasting my time and my life.

So since You *do* exist, I must finish what I've started.

I love You.

September 30, 2000; 4:20 a.m.; Chicago

My Love,

I feel very old and very fragile this Saturday morning with a trip to Europe just ahead of me. Part of it is that I had lunch with two people I had taught in grammar school back in the fifties. They obviously admired me after all these years, which may be a lot more than I deserved. In both cases, life had taken a lot out of them, though they were happy enough, in a humdrum sort of way.

I mourned for their loss of youthful enthusiasm and energy. I mourned for my failures with them. I mourned for my own mortality. I mourned for all my failures and losses.

Sad business, life. Also glorious.

I thought briefly of my own obituary as I quickly passed that page in the morning's paper. I wouldn't want to have to read it, because it would be like some of those nasty reviews and feature articles. I don't care much about that because I won't be around to read it. I'll be with You, You who love me no matter how much of a mess I have made of my life.

I try to love You in return.

October 1, 2000; 8:35 a.m.; Chicago

My Love,

October already!

I have completed the four key chapters in my book about religion in Europe, even if they kept me awake much of the night. My September target was fulfilled. One more chapter, and I'll be ready to work in preexisting materials. Thank You for helping me finish the task.

Archbishop Harry Flynn of St. Paul attacked me in his paper this weekend because of my *America* article. So it goes.

I still feel very fragile and old. Maybe if I could stop coughing I wouldn't feel old. On the other hand, maybe I should feel old!

Help me on this trip to Europe—on which I would rather not go.

I love You.

October 3, 2000; 7:30 a.m.; Chicago

My Love,

Not well this morning. Stomach as well as a cough. Minor stuff. Maybe rushing too much to get ready for the trip. Why am I going? I seem to have forgotten. Help me, please, to get through with it without falling apart.

I love You.

October 18, 2000; 8:20 a.m.; Chicago
My Love,

Fifteen days since I did one of these reflections. I think You understand why, and approve. More than that, I cannot say.

The trip was good, though I am exhausted—as I usually am after such ventures. Thank You for the trip. Thank You for bringing me home safely. Thank You for all your blessings and protections.

Grant peace to Mrs. Wallace and to Cliff, who prepared the trip so well.

Help me to get back into the routine in which spirituality is part of my daily life.

I love You.

October 19, 2000; 7:05 a.m.; Chicago
My Love,

So much of my spiritual problem comes from the lack of what they called in the seminary "recollection." I get carried away by the burdens and the responsibilities and the challenges of the day, and I forget about You. Surely that was the case during the trip. When I went into a church I prayed, but left the church without any awareness of your presence. That's stupid, isn't it? The trick, as I once learned, is to slip You into the interstices of the day, to recognize your presence while I'm waiting. Once more today, however belatedly in my life, I will try that again. Please help me.

I love You.

October 20, 2000; 7:30 a.m.; Chicago
My Love,

My heart is cramped with daily responsibilities, writing projects, obligations, cultural events, and now jet lag. There is no room for You in it.

Do saints suffer from jet lag? I suppose they do!

And what's the point of it all?

Not much. I do what I have to do, and don't do what would be better for me to do. I work on this book about religion in Europe, and I forget about You all day long.

Help me, I beg You, to do better on this lovely Indian summer day which is such a poignant reflection of both mortality and love.

I love You.

October 22, 2000; 8:45 a.m.; Chicago
My Love,

Last night was a strange mixture. A rather second-rate and even sleazy event, yet the people who showed up were deeply moving, especially three of my classmates. I almost wept when the crowd sang *Ad Multos Annos* with my classmates leading the singing.

I seem to be over the jet lag, mostly, and my bronchitis seems to be clearing up, for both of which many thanks.

I love You.

October 23, 2000; 8:55 a.m.; Chicago

My Love,

Mike Sveridoff's obit was in the *Times* this morning. Good man. Take him home in peace.

Joel Wells is dying. I will visit him later this week. Death all around.

I have the sense that I'm barely hanging on and still playing catch up.

I love You. Please take care of me.

October 24, 2000; 8:00 a.m.; Chicago

My Love,

Good night's sleep. Over the jet lag. Still not feeling well. I'm unsure as to whether this cold/bronchitis I have is a touch of pneumonia. I hope not. Take care of me, please. Help me to get my spiritual life straightened out. Just plain help me!

I love You.

October 25, 2000; 5:40 a.m.; Chicago

My Love,

So I get over the jet lag, but now I can't sleep, for the usual reasons! I was going to get up and go to the hospital to get a chest x-ray to exclude pneumonia. So naturally I woke up and couldn't go back to sleep—and now the fog is too dense to drive. So I'm going back to bed!

I continue to be a mess both physically and spiritually.

The new dean of students at the div school is Tom Faller's daughter. I met her last night at the visiting committee meeting. She brought back memories of that wonderful, wonderful man and strong ally. Also a saint. I'm sure he's home with You and watching over me as he did when he was alive.

I hope this lung business can be cleared up. If it can't, I accept your will. Help me to believe and act that way. I'm going back to bed now.

I love You.

October 26, 2000; 9:25 a.m.; Chicago

My Love,

The book is finished and at NORC being duplicated! Alleluia. It was the most difficult of all my sociological efforts because of the tedious detail of covering twenty-three countries on a couple score of variables. I think I did a pretty good job. For the whole effort, many thanks.

I acknowledge that my work was frantic. It was a new idea that I had to fit into my writing schedule. Instead of being sensible, I worked at it full blast. The date of my introduction was September 7. Now, seven weeks later, with twelve days out for the trip to Italy, a work of some sixty thousand words is finished. Kind of silly, I admit.

I experience a tremendous sense of relief, even exhilaration. That will last a day or two, and then I'll be busy with something else—the next Nuala Anne story, no doubt. I'll try to be more reasonable about it.

And I'll also get my spiritual life back on track.

I feel better physically, too.

I love You.

October 27, 2000; 7:10 a.m.; Chicago

My Love,

Back to work today on homilies and a Christmas newsletter and a column, as I try to catch up on the things I haven't done while I was in Italy and working on the book. Also, of course, Christmas presents. Run, run, run, run!

I'm trying to put a little recollecting back into my life, too. Not easy, especially this morning when I'm sedated by cough medicine.

Complain, complain, complain! I can hear You say it! Well, no, that's not what You say at all. You love me as your child, and You listen to my complaints with tolerant love.

As my life winds down, I regret even more the time I've wasted, the abysmal state of my prayer life, my failures. Most of them are caused by own desire to DO everything. Folly!

I'm sorry.

I love You.

October 28, 2000; 10:23 a.m.; Chicago

My Love,

A gray, quiet Saturday in Chicago, not gloomy, just gray. No wind. Church bells ring out clearly. No people in the streets yet. Our prolonged Indian summer is not quite over. Today is a cool interlude, an omen as Halloween approaches, of many, many gray days ahead. I kind of like today though. There is a beauty in grayness, the beauty of a sharp black-and-white print.

I'm reading a book of Celtic theology, a serious scholarly effort and not the kind of romanticism that is, alas, increasingly frequent. Today I learn about St. Patrick's sense of your overwhelming and mighty presence. I don't think he would have dared to presume such familiarity with You as these reflections pretend. I think I'm right; I think that, like all lovers, You delight in intimate familiarity. I think of Emily, the Brennan's dog, who last night decided she liked me and then curled up next to me on the couch, much to my delight. I didn't mind, and I'm sure You don't either, though the distance between me and You is much larger than between Emily and me.

Or is it? I'm not sure, and that doesn't matter. You want me to talk to You. I don't do it nearly enough. I'll keep trying.

I love You.

October 29, 2000; 7:50 a.m.; Chicago

My Love,

Brighter mornings, darker evenings. I don't like the trade!

Where did October go?

Where did my energy go? Why has everything lost its savor? Why must I force myself to work? Why do I want to do nothing but loaf and read?

Where, by the way, have You gone?

Or, as Peter Rossi used to say, has there been any good news in the last thousand years?

What's the matter with me this morning?

I need to recapture my energy and zip. Maybe I am really getting old. Maybe I ought to accept that and slow down.

Maybe.

I love You.

October 30, 2000; 8:30 a.m.; Chicago

My Love,

Busy morning. Phones.

I feel better, for whatever that's worth. Doctors tomorrow.

Big depression yesterday. Health, election. Maybe too much thought. Sorry.

Telephone interruption. NBC coming to ask me about the "Catholic vote." Nonsense.

I have to continue to be aware of your presence and to live in that presence. Please help me.

I love You.

November 1, 2000 (All Saints Day); 7:35 a.m.; Chicago

My Love,

Feast of all Saints and the temperature is 74. Wonderful. As I was driving home from the university this afternoon I observed the plume of Buckingham Fountain rising against the hazy sky—a kind of late defiance of the coming of winter. Impressive! Haiku material.

So much beauty in your creation!

> Fountain plume
> Feast of all the saints
> Hazy sky

I should go back to trying to do a haiku every day. I'll start again.

Still tired from yesterday's ordeal. Too much driving. Yet, I do feel better. Thank You.

I love You.

November 2, 2000; 8:50 a.m.; Chicago

My Love,

A gray, rainy All Souls Day. We inaugurate our new president at the university today. I'm going out for the lunch.

I am still tired, especially in the morning. Worn out, alas. Can't pray. Can't reflect. Can't mediate. Can still write, however. Maybe that's not a good thing.

A Norwegian stood up for me in the *Tablet*, defending *The Catholic Imagination*. That doesn't happen very often. My friends remain silent (as they always do), and a stranger defends me. Bless him!

I offer today for the souls in purgatory, in whatever sense that means to You.

I love You.

November 3, 2000; 7:46 a.m.; Chicago

My Love,

Much better today because of a good night's sleep. The wheeziness inside my skull have made for restless nights. Now that I know, courtesy of a doctor's call, that I have nothing but bronchitis, I slept a little better. Most of the sleep deprivation has been routed.

These have not been easy times. Considering what others my age must endure, though, I have little cause for complaint.

I was more aware of your presence during my attempt at contemplation this morning, the familiar sweet, happy sense of ambient love, of the presence of all the goodness and tenderness and joy in the cosmos touching me lightly, like a wife's touch on the cheek before going on to other tasks. The more I can recall such experiences, the better I will be able to live and serve You, and bring images of that love to the world.

That requires attention on my part and also health. A shame that the spirit must depend on the body, but it must.

Be with me during the day.

I love You.

November 4, 2000; 7:23 a.m.; Chicago
My Love,

A wasted Saturday already. Not a word done on the novel. Too many things to do. Will it ever stop? Tomorrow I must go to the Bears game! Faith or despair! Oh, well.

Daryl Strawberry of the Yankees in court on a drug charge, and with colon cancer, told the judge that he no longer had a desire to live. What a terrible story of great talent ruined by drugs, but even more by the viciousness of sportswriters who are some of the worst people in the world. Poor dear man, as the Irish would say. So much tragedy in life.

Life is finally tragic, isn't it? We all end badly, more or less. And it's your fault. Presumably You know what You're doing. Comedy finally trumps tragedy, doesn't it?

I hope so, in the strictest sense of the word.

And I love You.

November 6, 2000; 7:05 a.m.; Chicago
My Love,

Doctor visit today. All seems to be well—for which many thanks. Bronchitis much better. Will, indeed, probably plague me for the rest of my life. Election tomorrow and Christmas shopping begins. Let me enjoy the latter and tolerate the disappointment that the former will bring.

Help me to get over the tendencies toward hypochondria that I seem to be developing. What an idiot I would be if I got into that!

And help me to be aware of You and your love at all possible times, especially when listening to Mozart tonight.

I love You.

November 7, 2000; 7:47 a.m.; Chicago
My Love,

Election day. I have already given up because we're going to lose—and I don't much care. I hope we take Congress, but we won't know that until tomorrow morning, and I'm not giving up a night of sleep. No way.

Vienna symphony last night. Wonderful! Mozart (*Jupiter*)! I thought of You, at least occasionally. Thank You for the beauty. How can anyone possibly doubt? They do, of course. Who doesn't?—at least on occasion.

I'm going over to St. Joseph Hospital tomorrow to the neonatology floor to see all the little wonders You send us that medical science can now keep alive. How clever of them—and how clever of You.

I'll be looking forward to encountering grace—and lots of it.

I love You.

November 8, 2000; 8:11 a.m.; Chicago
My Love,

Well, I got a good night's sleep and didn't waste my time watching the election results, which are not in anyway. What a mess.

Article accepted for *American Journal of Sociology* yesterday. Victory of a sort. Somehow they don't matter anymore.

Nice sunny day. I'm off to see the neonates, who, as I said yesterday, are grace, your presence in the world supporting and celebrating life. I need grace today.

I continue to be dispirited. Excellent word. As if your Spirit has left me. I'm sure she hasn't. She never does. And I'm not so spiritually advanced that I can say it's a dark night. Rather, it's plain discouragement, weariness, and worry.

I should be ashamed of myself.

Still, I try to love You, I really do.

November 9, 2000; 8:35 a.m.; Chicago
My Love,

Presidential election is an absolute mess. Nineteen thousand ballots, most of them for Gore, disqualified in Florida. Long litigation and a tarnished presidency are inevitable. Country in trouble. Brought it on ourselves.

Wonderful grace at the hospital yesterday. Those little creatures are so wonderful. Young mother gently caressing her tiny son's back—so loving, so tender, so much like You. Or so I thought. And so it will be said in my novel.

I blessed both of them, avoiding tears with difficulty.

In such circumstances, how can anyone doubt You? They could say, of course, that You let those small ones be born early and cause suffering and tragedy for their families. But You will dry their eyes, too, as You dry everyone else's. A scene for poets and storytellers.

I love You.

(And bless the United States!)

November 10, 2000; 9:12 a.m.; Chicago
My Love,

Election crisis continues. A lot of terrible people saying terrible things. Bad news.

Memorial Mass yesterday was a curious experience. As the names of my dead classmates were read, I saw each of their faces and mourned them, though we will all be together again sometime. Some of them I didn't like at all, others I liked a lot, and others were close friends whom I miss desperately. Grant them all peace and rest and bring us together in happier times.

Only a few of us are still young, myself included. Does that sound arrogant? No, it's rather a statement of gratitude. If I am still alive and vital, part of the reason is the good health with which You have blessed me, despite my intermittent propensity toward hypochondria and the intellectual challenges You have put in my life. They interact with one another and I am very grateful for both.

Someday my name will be added to that list. Whenever You want it to be. Till then, I'll do my best.

I love You.

November 13, 2000; 8:30 a.m.; Chicago

My Love,

Back to CK for Mass and a lecture yesterday. A melancholy experience, not so much because of the familiar faces and bittersweet memories, but because the parish isn't what it used to be. Failures of leadership over many years has caught up with it. So sad.

Some of my friends said that the crowd at Mass doubled because I was there. Good news for my ego (and I discount their estimates), but bad news for the parish. A shame to see all the work of past years wiped out, but human efforts at the most will have only a transient impact. On the other hand, if one affects for your cause only a few people—through your grace— that is reason for rejoicing. Surely I have no right to expect that my own work would survive almost half a century.

Someone remarked recently that Jesus is rarely mentioned in my stories— a valid observation that scared me a little. Plenty about You, nothing or very little about your Son. I asked myself why. Part of the explanation is that I have been turned off by the misuse of Jesus in so much ideological propaganda, and part of it is I believe that the proper form of address is to You through him—but I don't even do that. I'll certainly work him into the current story. I can already hear Bishop Blackie talking about him.

I love You.

November 14, 2000; 8;05 a.m.; Chicago

My Love,

Cold here in Chicago today. Turned up the thermostat in my apartment (to 70) for the first time. One window vent won't close. Feels like my bronchitis is coming back! Ugh.

Saw *The Legend of Bagger Vance* yesterday. Another God-in-the-movies story. Not a great film but nicely done with some fine theological observations. Will Smith as You was a nice touch. None of the critics caught it, though Roger Ebert agreed when I e-mailed him. Why is it that the filmmakers know who You are but so many of the clergy do not?

Bagger says to the Matt Damon character at one point (first clear tip-off),

"I've always been with you and always will be." Who else but You?

Are You really with all of us? I think I have to believe that, though some people (surely not I) get shortchanged. Still, if You're You (and You are), then You must know what You're doing.

Good film. Thank You for it.

I love You.

November 18, 2000; 8:48 a.m.; Chicago

My Love,

Kind of took the morning off. Irresponsible. I've got to work on the novel.

Do You mind if I say something?

I'm tired of doing things I have to do. I'm tired of running. I'm even tired of doing these reflections each morning. You don't need them. I don't need them. Why bother?

I'm tired of e-mail. I'm tired of snail mail. I'm tired of the homilies. I'm tired of writing the column. I'm tired of everything. I don't want to go up to St. Mary of the Woods for Mass this afternoon. I don't want to go out for supper. I don't want to go Christmas shopping. I most especially don't want to go to Ireland on Wednesday. I don't want to come home to all the Christmas rush after Ireland.

I'm tired and I don't want to . . .

Don't think that I'm tired of living. I'm not. I'm merely tired of living the way I do. Change it, You say? Easier said than done.

Anyway I love You.

November 19, 2000; 7:55 a.m.; Chicago

My Love,

Well, the mayor flipped the switch last night and the lights went on all over the Mag Mile and environs, and the holidays are here five weeks before Christmas!

As You know, I have mixed feelings about holidays. For a priest (well, this priest anyway) they are a time of both loneliness and people overload. I hate Thanksgiving and don't mind being away in Ireland for it. People ask me, "Will you have a Thanksgiving supper with anyone on Thursday night?" I say, "Probably not." I don't add that I am thankful that I will not.

Christmas, the birth of your son as human, is another matter. It is a wonderful event, though I come home at the end dragged out and depressed.

What the holidays mean for me, I fear, is more of the same: more rushing, more demands, more harassment. Okay, Christmas is about giving and not getting. I give a lot (and I don't mean presents!) but I don't get much back. That should be all right for a priest, and I hope I continue to be generous.

However, in recent years it has not been much fun. But then neither has life. Like I said yesterday, I'm tired, though not as tired as I sounded then. I woke up as the day went on.

Well, the lights are on and I should set up my tree today, perhaps this evening, and begin to celebrate that life is stronger than death, love stronger than hate, and light stronger than darkness.

I love You, my Light.

November 20, 2000; 7:23 a.m.; Chicago

My Love,

Bitter cold day. Weather in Ireland can't possibly be this bad!

I continued to be discouraged, despite some nice letters this morning. Discouraged because I'm tired and old and so much of my efforts through the years have been wasted. Lost causes, most of them.

Mortality, too, impinges. At the most, I don't have much time left, do I? John Hayes sent me a funny letter to mark his seventieth anniversary in the priesthood. Told me to file it for 2024!

I won't live to my seventieth, pretty clearly. I'll be fortunate if I live to my fiftieth, not that anniversaries matter all that much.

I truly would like to retire from working, from sociology, from storytelling, from column writing, etc. But I won't. You know I won't, not as long as I have the strength to continue what I've started. I think this is the way You want me to be.

I love You.

November 22, 2000; 8:00 a.m.; Chicago

My Love,

Off to Ireland this evening. Great day here for flying. Maybe it won't be raining in Ireland. Train strike there. How do I get to Galway? Taxi! Strike is supposed to be over by Friday. Possible mess.

Please take care of me and protect me on the trip. Help me to perform credibly at the press conference in Dublin.

Tomorrow is our American Thanksgiving, which I will miss, and myself not missing it very much, if You take my meaning! However, I do what to thank You for my life and all the blessings in it. Help me not to cling to it too compulsively.

Yesterday, out on the Mag Mile in front of the Presbyterian church, I saw a mother kneeling on the ground in the bitter cold as she helped her son, somewhere between one and two put on his gloves (tied together by a string of course). He wasn't resisting, but he wasn't helping much either, mostly because he didn't know how. She was so patient and gentle with him, not at all troubled by the cold or the inconvenience of having a little one with her on a cold pre-Xmas shopping day. How like all mothers—or at least most mothers most of the time.

So You love me. Makes me want to cry, it's so tender. Help me to believe that, during my trip and always.

Why cling to life if one is held by such love?

There is a conspiracy. Everyone is telling me how good I look. People only do that when they've organized into a conspiracy based on the belief that poor Greels looks terrible so we must tell him how good he looks!

I'm kidding!

I love You.

December 2, 2000; 8:50 a.m.; Chicago

My Love,

Back from Erin's fair land. Rain and cold every day except the last one. Many adventures. I'm worn out now.

I love You.

December 3, 2000; 7:45 a.m.; Chicago

My Love,

I am depressed, as I always am after a trip across the ocean. I'm depressed because of death, depressed because I have such a sense of a wasted life, depressed because I have worked so hard and continue to work hard, with such little impact and with so much hatred.

So, You say, welcome to the club—which is the correct answer.

I think I operate on two levels, maybe everyone does. I feel that most of what I do is worthless and will end in death anyway. Then I continue to do what I think You want me to do regardless of how short time is. But what else is there to do?

I have Christmas music on now. It breaks my heart. So sweet and so wonderful and so transient.

Everything is transient.

As Sean McRaymond said in Dublin, there are only two absolutes in the world: a Finnish vodka and God's love! Help me to live and act as one should who believes that.

I love You.

December 4, 2000; 8:03 a.m.; Chicago

My Love,

There is a self-pitying article in the *Times* today by a novelist who laments that writing is a parallel world that interferes with the world of living. Leaving aside the self-pity and the narcissism, her point that writing brings one into a different world is true. Sure it does, that's the whole game. The writer entices the reader into an alternative world to illuminate him so that he can go back to the other world with enhanced possibilities for living. Maybe the author, if he has any sense, does the same thing.

As I struggle through *Irish Stew,* I am aware of how that other world takes hold of me and the characters become so very real and so poignantly powerful. It is a great gift to be a storyteller, and I'm thankful for it. Life would be so much easier if it were the only thing I do, but that is not the way things are or ever will be. I must make do.

But thanks again for the blessing. Help me to use it well.

I love You.

December 5, 2000; 8:35 a.m.; Chicago
My Love,

Twenty days till Christmas. Time running out, even if I have most of my shopping done. Christmas music, Christmas lights, Christmas candles, Christmas tree.

No Christmas spirit. Too much to do. Never any time. Run, run, run. Right into the grave.

Why do I work so hard? I can't believe You want me to work this hard, especially since there is so little payoff from it all. However, I'm caught in the treadmill and can't get off.

Anyway, I love You and I love Christmas.

December 6, 2000; 8:03 a.m.; Chicago
My Love,

I was up at 5:30 this morning to work on the novel before the phones began to ring. I managed to get three thousand words of my four thousand target done. No other way of working at this time of the year.

I've pretty well shaken off the effects of the jet lag.

I continue to be discouraged by the pile of obligations (including the novel) that piles up for me at this time of year. Work, work, work. Even the lunches and dinners are work. Many of them I don't want to do. No choice.

Complain, complain, complain, You might well say. I don't blame You, and I'm sorry. Some of it is being a priest and it goes with the territory. I harbor the illusion that it will be different when I get to Tucson. I'll settle and relax and read. But You know better than that—and so do I.

I'm going for the blood test tomorrow. I hope it's all right. I don't have time to be sick.

Sorry again for the complaints.

I love You.

December 7, 2000; 7:45 a.m.; Chicago

My Love,

New insight into me. I have an overload of compassion, perhaps of an unhealthy variety. It may come from being a novelist, or from having lived as long as I have. I see people and I want to protect them—little kids lined up for Santa Claus, for example, their eyes filled with wonder. I want to protect that wonder. Young parents walking along the Mag Mile, so careful and solicitous about their rug rats. Young priests with their ideals . . . on and on and on.

I can't protect them, of course, and the twist of pain I experience with that insight almost breaks my heart.

Who do I think I am? You?

No, not really, because You can't protect them either.

So I understand how You feel about all of us.

The difference is not that You are God and I am not. The difference is that You have promised to wipe away all our tears. I know You will do that. So when I feel that twist of pain, I know You experience something of the same, but You can take care of them, if only in the long run.

And of me, too.

I love You.

December 8, 2000; 7:30 a.m.; Chicago

My Love,

The jet lag lifted this morning, for which many thanks. There's no way to get around it—I need a week to shake the effects of an international trip. My thoughts and emotions and fantasies during that time are always weird. Maybe I shouldn't talk to You at all because I'm such a complaining nuisance! Or only say, "Hello, I'm a mess, I'm sorry." Also, the sun is out, which always helps me.

And I'm coming down the home stretch on the current novel, which also helps. I've been writing nonstop since early September. Lots of revisions needed, but it still kind of works, I think.

So a lot of the obligations slip away—and I feel better. I don't feel that my life has been a waste, though I regret that I have not been more aware of your presence.

Yet, I love You, I really do, and I will continue to try.

December 9, 2000; 8:00 a.m.; Chicago

My Love,

Novel finished, praise be to You! First revision pass today. I did the writing in separate times and places, so there may be a lot of work.

Thank You for blessing me with this talent.

Florida recount going on at last. Republican attempt to steal the election being frustrated. They are beginning to act crazy.

I feel so much better, for which many thanks. I know what kind of depression one gets into after a return from Europe, yet I never seem to be able to take it into account.

This is the last day of novel work or writing of any sort until next year! Thanks be to You again.

I love You.

December 10, 2000; 9:47 a.m.; Chicago
My Love,

I've done the first-pass editing on the novel and sent it off to my editor. It read better than I thought it would. I'm surprised I could juggle three such complex plots and not mess up more than I did. Again, many thanks.

I also slept through until 8:00 this morning, the first time I've done that in months. The burdens of the past months have been lifted. Now I must be careful not to slip into other work that will wear me down again.

Winter storm warning out there. Apartment is snug with Christmas music, candles, and trees.

I must now settle down into Christmas season—which I love.

And I love You.

December 11, 2000; 5:05 p.m.; Chicago
My Love,

The city is covered with a foot of snow, the winds are sweeping off the lake at 40 miles an hour, and ordinary human life slows down. Mine less for some odd reason. Even though the novel is done, I get to this reflection at 5:00 p.m. A day of running, pointless most of it, but necessary. I haven't even had time to turn on the Christmas music.

I pray for all those who are out in the cold—cops, snow removal people, transit workers, fireman, etc. Where would we be without them?

It is astonishing how human ingenuity copes with these problems. By tomorrow the city will be working again. What was it like in the days of Ned Fitzpatrick in my novel? The city shut down, I suppose, and took a few more days to bounce back. More people froze to death. Thank You for the progress.

I had a cry from the heart on e-mail from folks with genetic illness in their families. Wonder why You do it? I assured them that You didn't. Probably not much help because they have been taught otherwise. Help them. Help all the poor people who write to me.

I love You.

December 12, 2000; 8:45 a.m.; Chicago
My Love,

Still bitter cold and strong wind. And myself going out every night this week! An attempt at reconciliation tonight. Hope it works. Must not lose my temper. Must be firm.

Trying to put my books in order, to figure out what I will read in Tucson. I was reluctant to leave Chicago until winter came. Now I'm in a rush.

Ice clings to my windows like some kind of translucent bug.

Hard to slow down after four months of hard work and travel. I must put some efforts into it.

Still no ruling from the Imperial Court. Had lunch with Marty. Many memories from the past. Can't be preserved, though my books do it in some ways.

I love You.

December 13, 2000; 8:25 a.m.; Chicago
My Love,

The Supreme Court stole the election for Bush. Bad news for the country. I am now going to write something and then erase it, so that it will never risk being in print but will be saved on the hard disk of your knowledge alone.

I love You.

December 14, 2000; 8:55 a.m.; Chicago
My Love,

I am a little ashamed of myself this morning. I was on display at dinner last night, and I slipped into the habit of being the oracle, the wise man, the expert for the younger clergy there, good men and true. I knew I was doing it after awhile, but it was too late to wiggle out of it. I'm sorry. I feel like a bit of a fraud.

The only thing worse than not being taken seriously is to be taken seriously! I'll try not to do it again.

I love You.

December 16, 2000; 8:25 a.m.; Chicago
My Love,

More snow. I skidded into a snowbank last night to avoid a big lamppost. Thank You for putting the snowbank there!

I ponder the fact that I no longer find the Christmas stories appealing. I have the candle and the trees lit and the crib displayed and the music playing, and I like all these things, but the Bethlehem story no longer seems fresh and alive. My fault? Or repetition? Probably. Also, I'm still running, even though the novel is finished. I must try to reflect on it more in the nine days that remain.

I love You.

December 18, 2000; 8:50 a.m.; Chicago
My Love,

The *Messiah* was wonderful yesterday. I just let the words and the music wash over me, with little effort to follow along. I don't know whether that was right or wrong, but it was all I could do—and it was nice. Maybe my spiritual burnout is even worse than I thought.

I do need time and quiet. Even finishing the novel pretty definitively doesn't seem to have relaxed me as much as I had hoped.

The words "I know that my Redeemer liveth" keep resonating in my mind. I do know that. I know that Jesus lives, and I know that You live and that I will live, too. I must hang on to that truth and to You as the Christmas carols play in the background, celebrating.

Celebrating what? Victory! Of love over hate! Of light over darkness! Of peace over conflict! Of life over death!

That's what the carols are about. That's what the *Messiah* is about. That's what Christmas is about. It confirms the deep-rooted human instinct, eradicable, that good is stronger than evil and that all matter of things will be well.

I believe that. Help me to believe that more strongly than ever during this Christmastime.

I love You.

December 21, 2000; 8:15 a.m.; Chicago
My Love,

First day of winter. Shortest day of the year. Bitter cold. Snow. We've had winter for two weeks. I'm fed up with it. Spoiled, I guess, by my ability to escape it all and run off to Tucson.

Must go to the university today, fight snow and slippery streets.

I am truly tired. Rough quarter.

Also, as You certainly know, burned out spiritually. All my own fault. Help me to rekindle myself in the days ahead.

I love You.

December 22, 2000; 7:55 a.m.; Chicago
My Love,

I am overwhelmed by STUFF! Presents, cards, gifts to bring, places to be, things to do—clutter, clutter, clutter! Too much! My whole life symbolized by one apartment in which I am being gradually pushed into the center by all the STUFF around me.

I'm also tired again, even though I have done nothing for the last couple of weeks except contend with clutter and run off to lunches, dinners, and parties!

I need to sleep, and there is no time to sleep, not really to sleep.

I need to slow down, as I hope to do when I get to Tucson, but I know I won't.

I opened my Christmas cards today. What a strange life I have led. One letter denounced me for advertising my books in my mailbox parish newsletter, and wondered how much money I made on the books! Great Christmas message! Oh well.

Most of them, however, were works of love, though it is a shame that Christmas cards have to be a burden to so many people. They are nonetheless an attempt at sending love, and should be appreciated and celebrated. Obligations? Yes. Doesn't everything become an obligation. Yet, it is still love, and for the love in the cards I am grateful.

Help me to keep my temper in the difficult days ahead.

I love You.

December 24, 2000 (Christmas Eve); 5:15 p.m.; Chicago

My Love,

It's 5:15 on Christmas Eve, and I'm still rushing. The day of recollection went down the drain when I agreed to go out to St. Angela for a Mass the cardinal was saying for the parish. That emotional experience was perhaps just as good as a day of recollection (now postponed till December 30, with your help).

In the low sunlight of the bitter cold day, the neighborhood was bathed and cleansed and looked so beautiful. The church, despite some leaking plaster, is still magical. The memories were generally benign, though some of the images that flashed through my mind were sad or painful.

I received a note from a classmate with her Christmas card. Her husband had died in the spring, painfully she said, of prostate cancer, and she had undergone a hip replacement. I remember so very clearly as though it were yesterday, encountering them on a bus from Fox Lake when they were courting—the joyous expectations at the beginning of love and the pain at the end.

Take care of them both, I beg You. Wipe away all their tears and refresh their love.

We all die painfully and sadly. Take care of us, too.

Help me to remember in the insane rush of tomorrow that You are the God of light and life and love.

I love You.

December 26, 2000; 8:48 a.m.; Chicago

My Love,

Yesterday was a nightmare. I was a shambles at the end of the day. I will not go into the details because You know them even better than I do. Christmas really didn't happen. Moreover, I'm in no position today to complain, lest I break people's hearts. But it was awful.

I don't understand . . . Well, maybe I do. I don't understand how I should respond, however. Probably there is no way other than keeping my mouth shut—which I did. It was so ugly.

Well, nothing more to say today. I'm worn out, battered, and depressed.

I love You.

December 30, 2000; 8:35 a.m.; Chicago

My Love,

I am very grateful still to be alive and still to have a car. As You well know, because your mother and the angels were working overtime—and St. Christopher, even if he doesn't exist. I plowed into a snowbank on the way to Clarendon Hills last night, and three state police cars and a tow truck were required to free me. Scary, scary experience.

Trouble was, the ramps on I-94 are not well designed and are upon you before you know it. There was so much snow I couldn't distinguish between the ramp and the highway, and ended up in between. I was able to drive home after dinner with only moderate nervousness.

Thank You much for giving me yet another chance at life.

Christmas has been a washout. On the other hand, I did spend most of my time trying to represent You for others, no matter how badly I did it. Right now I am very tired and want to get out of here to Tucson, where I plan to read and maybe do some poetry to get back into the proper spiritual rhythms.

Help me please.

I love You.

— *2001* —

January 1, 2001 (New Year's Day); 8:40 a.m.; Chicago

My Love,

There's supposed to be something magical about 01/01/01. Actually, it is the beginning of a new millennium—for which new beginnings and new graces I thank You.

I thought that Christmas would be a time of grace. In fact, as I might have expected from the past, it is a time of weariness and exhaustion. I can hardly think, I'm so tired. I beg You to help me relax these weeks ahead in Tucson.

I love You.

January 7, 2001; 7:30 a.m.; Tucson

My Love,

The *NYT* magazine today had its annual collection of hip obits, some nasty, some derisive, some tender, some celebratory—many smart-mouth. They made interesting reading if one wanted to meditate on the shortness of life and the ephemeral nature of fame. How easy it is for both a clever journalist and an articulate friend (or enemy) to sum up the hopes and the fears, the joys and the sorrows, the pains and the survivals of a human life. I think the *Times* custom is finally despicable because it gives so many people opportunities to settle scores.

I hate to think what my obits will be like, but then I won't be around so it won't matter when I'm home with You.

One tries, and then there is oblivion and then new life.

Lots of dreams. I'd forgotten about my Tucson dreams, how haunted and spectacular they usually are—and occasionally illuminating. I have dreamed about my first love—which ended in third grade when we moved, though she was still in our class in grammar school. I have already recreated her in a story, and still grieve for her after all these years. I hope she is happy, wherever she is. In the dream, as in the story, I tried to save her, something I would not have had the courage to do then, if there had been a chance—which there wasn't.

Well, we will meet again. We will love again. We will laugh again.

And thank You for bringing her into my life, if only for a brief interlude.

I love You.

January 8, 2001; 8:00 a.m.; Tucson

My Love,

Still having strange dreams. Or perhaps only more aware of them. Shifting rectories again in the city and the diocese, which my dreamworld has created. The repeated dream about the assignment that takes away my role at the university. That happened thirty-six years ago. Why does it still come back? Perhaps because my position in the archdiocese (and the city and the university) is still in doubt, perhaps because I am still the invisible man.

I was upset about that once again over the weekend (foolishly). I should forget about it and celebrate my freedom. I'm sorry.

I love You.

January 15, 2001; 7:40 a.m.; Tucson

My Love,

I worry about little girls. They seem to be the happiest people on earth. Yet, their happiness is so often destroyed as they grow up. Through much of human history, they have been the victims of men's lust and cruelty. Even now, their happiness and their desire for love is so often blighted by stupid, gross, and insensitive men. It's not fair. Whenever I see a cute little kid bouncing along after her mother in the supermarket, I want to grieve because I know how much she is likely to have to suffer.

You must do something about it. I realize that You are, and I regret that the Church is so tardy in its concerns. We are run by the same kind of men that mess up the lives of women they marry.

I must say something about this sometime soon.

I love You.

January 21, 2001; 8:05 a.m.; Tucson
My Love,

A quiet, sunny Sunday morning in Tucson. I am discouraged both by the Bush inaugural and with the list of new cardinals. Things do not arrange themselves well, not at all.

Also about mortality. Being discouraged about it does not change it, any more than my discouragement changes the reality of who's running the Church and the country.

Three weeks here in Tucson. I am more relaxed and I sleep better, but I'm still spiritually exhausted. I really have to meditate and reflect more. So many things cross my mind as I read the poetry each day. I'm dull, insensitive, hurried—no way for a man to be who has, at the most, a few more trips to Tucson in his life.

I am so sorry. For what? I don't know! For everything. For all that I've wasted. For worrying. For becoming angry. Sorry for everything. For my foolish doubts, too.

I love You.

January 22, 2001; 8:25 a.m.; Tucson
My Love,

A poet I was reading yesterday noted that all the furniture around him would surely survive him. He kind of hoped that his lamp would show up at his gravesite. Very Irish, comedy and despair. Also very true. This house, the pool, the new furnace, this computer—all have greater durability than I do. Well, maybe not the computer!

Yet, it is true, isn't it?

I hope that when I die, I die as a man of faith, as someone who truly believes. Yet, one doesn't get much choice in the matter, does one? Anyway, the secret is to live as a man of faith and trust in You. Not much choice there either.

Yet, as I was driving home from a movie last night and thinking about the malt I was going to buy, I had a kind of epiphany. A malt after a film is a good thing. In a world where there is such goodness (minor as it may be) there are grounds for hope. So today I'm upbeat.

Back to Chicago tomorrow for a crazy week. Take care of me, I beg You. *I love You.*

February 3, 2001; 7:50 a.m.; Tucson

My Love,

Missed St. Brigid's Day. Sorry. Festival of Brigid, Purification, Candlemas, and Groundhog! I honor herself, of course. All in some fashion, feasts of spring and new life. Well worth celebrating new life as I slowly rout this cold.

My mood is mercurial, mostly because of the cold and because the waves of insights that overwhelm me and which I am unable to pull together. I must do this poem or sequence sometime soon.

Often, as I approach my seventy-third birthday, I lament the waste of my life, not in terms of production—there has been much of that. But in terms of my spiritual development. Yet, I know You love me, and that's what counts. As I prepare for death, whenever it comes, I must hold on to your love. Help me never to let it go.

I love You.

February 4, 2001; 7:40 a.m.; Tucson

My Love,

A friendly letter from a fellow priest to meditate on as my seventy-third draws close:

It's a good thing for you that I am not your boss, because I would make you the pastor of the very worst parish in the diocese (no money, lots of debt, a declining membership, etc.).

Did you ever minister to the people of the diocese? Or have you always lived a life of splendor at the John Hancock Tower, wrote trashy novels, and associated with the high-powered people and high-profile scum of this country?

So while other priests are overwhelmed ministering to "the flock," you are totally comfortable being totally removed from "the flock."

I have to give you credit for knowing how to take care of #1 . . . no stress, no pain . . . just a life of luxury. I wonder if God will have mercy on your chosen pathetic life????

Obviously he knows nothing about me or my life or my work. The letter tells more about him than it does about me. Yet, I must realize that most priests think the same thing about me, though perhaps in less violent fashion (and sometimes more violent).

I am surprised, though perhaps I shouldn't be. Why bother even writing such a note? What good does it do him, other than provide a temporary release from his anger and frustration? I did not expect reactions like this from priests when I started. Now they don't surprise me at all. If I had known that I would become an outcast, would I have done anything differently?

Surely not. So I have no grounds for complaint. Yet, it is not pleasant to have such vomit poured out. It goes with the territory. I feel sorry for him and all like him.

And I regret permitting myself to be disturbed even transiently. That's merely the way it is.

You put up with a lot worse.

I love You.

February 5, 2001; 8:10 a.m.; Tucson
My Love,

Seventy-three years! Thank You for all of them!

They have been interesting years. Among the things I can remember which most people today can't: Pearl Harbor, the death of Roosevelt, the Missile Crisis, the Kennedy assassination . . . Remember in the sense of knowing exactly where I was and what I was doing when it happened.

The best way to look at it all is that I have piled up experiences that few people ever will: the Depression, World War II, post-war, the Second Vatican Council, the changing Church. I hope I have learned something from them. I hope that they have been experiences and not just things that happened.

I thank You for the gift of life, for my parents, for my family, for my faith, for the Church, for the priesthood, for my teachers, my friends, for those who have loved me or love me still.

I'm sorry for all my complaints, for the wasted opportunities, for the anger, for not being joyful enough or grateful enough, for the prayers I have not said. I ask You to bless me and protect me in the years ahead, and to help me to become a better person, the kind of person You gave me life that I might be.

Also, help me to shake the ill effects of this cold, so I can respond to the celebrations of this week.

I love You.

February 7, 2001; 8:00 a.m.; Tucson
My Love,

When I was younger I often wondered if I would live till the end of the millennium. That would mean I'd be seventy-two years old—which I still was last month. Since most of my relatives didn't last that long, I really didn't expect it. Life expectancies changed and maybe I picked up some of the long-lived genes of past ancestors on both sides. So here I am, seventy-three and in the third millennium. Big deal!

But one way to look at it would be that survival into the new millennium is a big surprise and that everything from now on is pure gravy, pure gift, pure grace. Everything, of course, is pure grace, life itself to begin with. However, it is useful spiritually (perhaps) to use this perspective and keep telling myself that from now on it is, to change the metaphor, ice cream on the cake.

For which many thanks.

I love You.

February 12, 2001; 7:50 a.m.; Tucson

My Love,

The week of birthday partying is over. It was fun, I guess, and one should celebrate birthdays, I guess. Yet, it was not so much fun that I was ecstatic about it. My reluctance to engage in such celebrations continues. In fact, I find them a drag. However, I suspect You would mildly disapprove of my negative feelings. I should celebrate, should I not, the life and health You have given me?

I continue to ponder the possibility of not writing any more novels. Quit when you're ahead, says I. All I really want to do is sit and do nothing but read. Somehow the fun seems to have gone out of writing—maybe out of everything else. Or maybe this is just a gloomy Monday with a busier week, indeed two weeks, ahead that I would like.

Anyway I love You—and thanks for the birthday and the birthday week.

February 14, 2001; 7:20 a.m.; Tucson

My Love,

Two themes occupy me today: 1) My wasted spiritual life and 2) tragedy. All these years a priest and all the efforts I've put into it (periodically at any rate) and my abilities at prayer are nonexistent. And the tragedy I see facing little kids, especially little girls who are more enthusiastic (on the average) than little boys and who dream bigger dreams.

I'm sorry about the former. It's mostly my fault. I am too much involved in the world. Maybe I should seriously try to pull back—if I can.

As to the latter, that's mostly your fault. Why do You create beings who are capable of big dreams if those dreams are only to be dashed? I think of the people I knew who were growing up when I worked at CK. So much disappointment, so much tragedy, so much heartache. Looking back at those days, it was all unnecessary, at least in the broader sense of that word. I tried, but my task was impossible. I don't blame myself, though. As someone from that era once said, I didn't cause their failure, I merely heightened their guilt feelings.

None of this leads anywhere, but I still feel the need to say that I'm sorry. *I love You.*

February 16, 2001; 8:00 a.m.; Tucson
My Love,

I have spent the last couple of days mostly reading three books—John Shelton Reed's story about Anglo-Catholicism, *The Rynville Letters* of the Gogarty Family, and Gary Giddins's remarkable book about Bing Crosby. All three leave me sad because they illustrate the folly of human effort and the sadness of human deterioration.

The Anglo-Catholics mostly won their fight for more Catholic ritual and doctrine in the Anglican Church, a vain attempt, as I see it, to restore the analogical imagination in Anglicanism, yet their efforts did not transform the Church so that it could win back its people.

There was so much love and so much hope and so much suffering in the Gogartys, especially during the war, and yet in the end they all were unhappy and died as we all must. Reading their letters makes them much more alive than if I were reading biographies. In this age of e-mail and telephones, such collections of letters will be infrequent.

Crosby, after a couple decades of contempt, is not hailed as the great (if oddly insecure) person he was. Why was there so much abuse of him? Why so much hatred? Is that what comes of success? It doesn't detract from his happiness now, but it is ugly and evil.

All of this fits with my current mood that all things are vanity.

Except your love.

I love You.

February 17, 2001; 8:55 a.m.; Tucson
My Love,

The Bing Crosby bio was truly amazing. In this day, when most biographies are intended to destroy the reputation and the memory of the one whose story is being told, Gary Giddins clearly likes Bing and wants to present him as the generally admirable person he was. Astonishing! And from the *Village Voice* at that.

Giddins is a truly generous, open-hearted man. There should be more writers like him. I should be so lucky to have someone like him write about me.

Truth is, Bing couldn't have cared less when he was alive, and surely doesn't now since he's at home with You.

Maybe I'm wrong there. Maybe he feels happy about the book. Why wouldn't he?

Teach us to care and not to care.
I love You.

February 18, 2001; 8:10 a.m.; Tucson
My Love,
   More reflections on Bing.
   It is astonishing to me how much competitiveness and envy he stirred despite his graciousness and generosity. His brothers, his wife, his friends, even some of his sons found themselves in constant competition with him, along with accompanying resentment. What can a person do when his most intimate role-opposites set themselves in competition with him? Bad scene. Why is this kind of competition necessary? Is the capital sin of envy that deep?
   Why should I think I'm unique when the same thing happens to me—and I am much less talented than Bing?
   Is it all right with You if I say I hate it?
   I love You.

February 24, 2001; 8:50 a.m.; Chicago
My Love,
   Back in Chicago for a wedding, opera, concert, etc. Cold is better but not gone by any means. I'm tired from all the travel but not as tired as I expected. Filled with a sense of the tragedy of life.
   I love You.

February 25, 2001; 9:20 a.m.; Chicago
My Love,
   I just wrote a column about genome research in which I bet that it would not eliminate the wonder and the mystery and the surprise from our lives (and that the fruit flies and the roundworms were not about to overtake us).
   I believe this like I believe everything. But I can't taste it, feel it, exult in it. On the contrary, I had nightmares, many of them last night, which were all grim and depressing. Maybe it's my lingering cold or weariness from all the traveling. I don't know. I do know that I am in a grim frame of mind. I cover it up nicely, but the joy seems to have gone out of life. Surely my sense of my own mortality has something to do with this. Also the weakness of my prayer life and a feeling that I have wasted much of my life.
   I have to do something about this, but I don't know what it is. Please guide me and direct me.
   I love You.

February 28, 2001 (Ash Wednesday); 8:25 a.m.; Tucson
My Love,

Back in Tucson, thanks be to You. These weeks of running around the country are deadly. Now I have only the three days in Chicago at the end of March, and all of that will be in the seminary. No more of this stuff from now on.

Some Lenten resolutions: these reflections get done first thing in the morning. No desserts, at least when I'm alone. Help me to keep them.

Clean bill of health from the doctors. Better health than is typical for my age. For which many thanks. I know I don't deserve it.

I find once again a need to try to integrate my life. It's been six years since I wrote *Furthermore*. Not enough has happened to require or even permit another memoir. So perhaps I will try some poetic, symbolic effort. Right now I feel a failure again, at least a spiritual failure. That is surely true, but not the whole truth. Maybe some poetry will tie things together and grant if not exactly more peace at least a sense of . . . of what? I don't know.

Yet, I still love You.

March 1, 2001; 8:40 a.m.; Tucson
My Love,

My life goes on at two levels. On the first, I am doing my usual work, sociology, fiction, journalism. On another level, I am examining my life and finding it wanting, a life made up of trajectories of my usual work. At the same time, I am in constant mental dialogue with those who hate me. I am, for example, preparing an article on priestly work that will stir up the haters again, and I am already thinking of my responses, which, if I am wise, I will not make.

Quite a mess, isn't it? Especially since much of the resentment against me is that I have been such a success!

There is something missing in all of this, something that I don't see. At least I think there is. At any rate, I must try to pray more and to reflect more and to be more honest with myself.

Help me to see.
I love You.

March 2, 2001; 8:00 a.m.; Tucson
My Love,

My dreams often turn into a review of my past life, often mourning for what is lost. In my waking hours I look back on stupid mistakes, made generally from an excess of zeal and concern.

Mistakes are part of the human condition. No one is immune. I'm not sure that mine were any worse than anyone else's. Nor that the others involved in many of the mistakes were totally innocent. I meant well, but that's not enough. Nor, alas, can they be undone. I've tried and it hasn't worked.

Sad.

Even now I don't understand.

I tried, perhaps too hard.

At least I haven't made those mistakes again.

I love You.

March 3, 2001; 8:30 a.m.; Tucson

My Love,

I did a bad thing last night: I worked till 10:00, and of course I couldn't sleep. The new Blackie book is haunting me, too.

The poems I read yesterday seem to emphasize the importance of seizing beautiful moments as evanescent as they may be. I reflect on the times I've sat through operas and concerts and have been preoccupied by other things. What a goof!

Help me to avoid that in the future and to seize the moments of beauty in the AZ sunshine and wherever else they may intrude in my life, bringing your grace and your love.

Help me in those moments, especially to return your love.

March 4, 2001; 9:35 a.m.; Tucson

My Love,

Last night as I was going to be bed, my head filled with ideas for poems, articles, books, chapters, Blackie interludes, columns—a creative imagination run amok. Where will I get the time to do all of them or even some of them? I have the sense of falling behind.

All my life I have been preaching, a ministry of word that is also, I hope, a ministry of *The Word*. A lot of people listen, a lot don't—especially those I wanted to influence: church leaders, priests, fellow social scientists. I have continued to try and thus to bang my head against the wall. So what! It is my mission, my vocation, I think, to try to be heard. If they don't hear me, and of course they don't, that's their problem. If they won't hear, and they won't, then that is not my problem. In doing this, have I spread myself too thin? Yes, of course I have, but that seems to be the kind of person I am, the sort of person You made me.

As I continue this problematic attempt to make sense of my life, I must remember that I am what You made me and that You love me as I am—though You want me to be more. If in some ways I have wasted my talents, lost opportunities, it was not altogether my fault, and You understand and

love me just the same. I am your beloved child. Help me never to forget that.
I love You.

March 5, 2001; 9:05 a.m.; Tucson

My Love,

I read half of Bernard Häring's little memoir last night. It brought back all of the excitement at the time of the council, and made the present situation in the Church look even worse than I had appreciated. We are still into the posture of trying to control the lives of the faithful, those who, as the *Catechism* says, are under "law and authority." The people on top don't get it. There is no law or authority anymore, not in their sense. Authority is nothing more than a license to practice charm and persuasion. I wonder how many priests realize that. Perhaps not too many. You can give orders till you're blue in the face (or crimson), and it won't do any good. We have lost it, for weal or woe. Blind obedience is dead. It will not rise. Nor, in my judgment, should it.

We are in an era of great tension and strain. It will go on for a long time. Church leadership is making it more difficult.

I hope my stories help the transition. I must keep that in my mind as I work on my next story. A cardinal's visit to the White House while Blackie is there. Fun, but the point must be made.

Also, the point that Mike Leach makes on the tape I listened to yesterday: people won't leave the Church.

I love You.

March 6, 2001; 8:35 a.m.; Tucson

My Love,

As I think back on my life (a mistake perhaps), I realize that this melancholy about what I have done is not new; I've always felt I was a failure. The added dimensions now are a sense of spiritual failure and the sense that time is running out.

If my writing has turned more acerbic (and funnier), the reason may be the bitterness that comes from failure.

We have been through this before, You and I. If I am marginal to all my professions, it's because I've been true to my vocation and refused to compromise. Rather than say that, which might be self-serving, I never thought of being anything different. I wouldn't do any of that differently.

It's the spiritual failure that bothers me the most. Yet, maybe You've designed me in such a way that I'm supposed to be always trying. Then I must continue to try and continue to fail.

I don't know. I won't stop trying, however.

I love You.

March 7, 2001; 7:55 a.m.; Tucson
My Love,
   Rain! Ugh!
   I continue to read Häring's book. He argues that much of the quasi restoration of the last twenty years is an attempt to control the lives of the people and especially their sex lives. Hard to disagree. Alas, despite the repression in the Church, the embarrassment of the laity, the losses to the Church, it has been counterproductive. That's what happens when the leadership gets divorced from the real world. It's not been a good time in Catholicism. How many wasted opportunities!
   A good time for me, however, because I'm a marginal person. Theologians like Häring were much more on the spot.
   The pope, it is said, is furious at the resistance to his will, to the work of counter-magisterium, as he called it. However, he has it wrong. It's not the theologians; it's the ordinary laity, the "simple" so loved by Cardinal Ratzinger, who have revolted.
   Well, there's nothing I can do about it. I write my stories about Catholic life, hope for change—which I am not likely to see—and lament the terrible losses.
   I love You.

March 8, 2001; 7:25 a.m.; Tucson
My Love,
   Cheerful music, sun breaking through the clouds. Time for me to take cheer, to enjoy the gifts of life and love and purpose and talent You have bestowed upon me. Whose are the voices I hear in my head? Envious fellow priests? Unimaginative sociologists? Nasty reviewers? Why do I listen to them and not to the many people who see me differently? I dunno. I should know better, but I don't. I guess I want approval from those from whom I will never get it.
   My one real regret continues to be spiritual. However, as I figured out (again) yesterday, the secret is to try—and that I will surely do.
   I worry about the country this morning. The president blows off all the work done with North Korea, Congress passes a bill repealing occupational health and safety measures. Greed is here to stay. Well, I must denounce that as best I can.
   As for the state of the Church, I do and have done my part. There's no more I can do. I must therefore try to enjoy the blessings of life and thus be grateful for your love.
   I do love You!

March 9, 2001; 8:40 a.m.; Tucson
My Love,

Off to see the Cubs and the Sox today. No excuse for it except hospitality. I continue to work hard but also to take time off. Maybe that doesn't require an excuse.

I love You.

March 10, 2001; 8:15 a.m.; Tucson
My Love,

I have been struggling these last few days with the poems of Wendell Berry, usually reading them two or three times before I figure out what he's saying. I think about writing more poetry, but am intimidated by the excellence of poets like him. He's much concerned, as I am, with light and darkness. In a poem I read last night, he suggested that we are the light that we cannot see, light for others but not for ourselves because we don't realize that we are light.

If I am to judge by my e-mail, I have been light for many people. Strange that I do not take such mail more seriously. Perhaps the impact of the haters and the liars has inoculated me against such positive reactions. That's giving away too much, isn't it?

I do reflect the light of the world, your light, to many people. I must respect that light and find hope in it.

Terrible dreams last night about a promotion tour, all because I have a radio interview ten minutes away from here on Monday! Silly.

I love You. Help me to understand that I am light.

March 11, 2001; 8:55 a.m.; Tucson
My Love,

Read a lot of Irish poetry last night. Yeats was truly a genius. His wonderful poem about Father Peter Gilligan (and You) was deeply moving. Maybe simple priests like Peter were better off than very complex ones like me.

I'm down this morning for a whole of reasons. More of that feeling of waste. I'll get over it.

I love You.

March 14, 2001; 7:25 a.m.; Tucson
My Love,

Practice resurrection, the poet tells me this morning. What a wonderful idea, especially when you're exhausted from a wonderful trip to Mexican shrines yesterday, for which many thanks.

So I must practice resurrection all day long.

I love You.

March 15, 2001; 9:20 a.m.; Tucson
My Love,

Richard Wilbur writes a poem to St. Lucy this morning that says in effect that the eyes should not deceive us as to the quality of a person. At the same time, I read in the paper that beautiful babies get better care than ugly babies. Wilber is so right, isn't he? While we admire beauty in a person, we ought not let that determine everything. Indeed, external appearances are not the whole story and, finally, only a small part of it. Even the pest or angry writer are your children and should be loved as best as one can. I must be aware of this insight and do my best to honor it.

I love You.

March 19, 2001; 9:55 a.m.; Tucson
My Love,

I'm reading some of Paul Murray's poems this week. They remind me of the many poems I have not written because I've been pressed so hard by so many "obligations." He refers to the "gift"—the sudden idea that fills out a paper, the sudden insight that finds the right word or the right line for a poem, the sudden response to a troubled friend. Or, as I would add, the sudden insight on how to write a scene or the sudden insight about a variable to use in analysis or the sudden explosion of a plot in a novel.

They are indeed gifts, which is why the ancients believed in muses. More seriously, they are explosions of the creative imagination—the agent intellect—as it roams around, not completely under our control.

There is something God-like—You-like—in that gift. You don't intervene with the variable for analysis, but You did create us this way, which helps us share in the intuitiveness of your knowledge. A precious gift, both in its individual instances and in its overarching power. Thank You.

I love You.

March 20, 2001; 9:05 a.m.; Tucson
My Love,

Rather than spend a couple of hours wandering in the desert looking at wild flowers (best in last ten years), I went to the Tucson Botanical Gardens to see them in concentrated form. It was a great experience. How brilliant of You to think of flowers, and in such a superabundant variety at that. I understand the ecological role of flowers and the evolutionary process. I realize that science can "explain them," that they are the result of precise algorithms. Yet, none of this finally accounts for the beauty which science tends, in effect, to explain away.

Science cannot make the beauty any less beautiful. Faced with such beauty, one turns to other forms of knowledge and thinks of Beauty. Where there is beauty there must be Beauty. Where there is so much beauty in such incredible variety there must be spectacular Beauty. This is not so much proof as hint, illustration, sacrament.

Thank You for the beauty and for the grace of the visit to the garden and for the people who left their home to the city of Tucson. So much color and grace.

I love You.

March 21, 2001; 8:35 a.m.; Tucson

My Love,

A friend of mine who thought that he was in good health and that everything was fine in his life has been diagnosed with cancer—a variety that does not make the situation look terribly hopeful. As he said, his whole life changed in a single day. I pray that You are able to give him complete recovery and prospects for a longer life.

I also reflect that this is the nature of the human condition, at a certain age in life or indeed at any age in life. The same thing can happen to me and arguably will. When it happens, help me to act like a follower of yours should.

We are all doomed to die and most deaths are messy. Grant me faith and patience and fortitude.

And faith in your love all the time.

I do love You.

March 26, 2001; 7:40 a.m.; Tucson

My Love,

David Tracy's lectures at Mundelein were superb—all about You, the Impossible, the Incomprehensible. Any God worth anything would be both impossible and incomprehensible, which in David's theology are positive terms. You are totally beyond our understanding, not merely because we have limited minds but because it is of your essence to be Impossible.

Or Overwhelming, as I would say it. Something else altogether. A firestorm of knowledge and love. I love that!

And I love You.

I am dead tired this morning from the last four days of wandering.

But I still love You.

March 27, 2001; 8:00 a.m.; Tucson

My Love,

I was greatly discouraged again last night, feeling that somehow my life is a waste, when of course it isn't. Part of the reason was the ads I read about summer programs. I never went to any of those, never even seriously thought about them. None of them offered me anything I didn't know. The Tracy lectures the other day were worth scores of summer programs. Yet, I remembered that, in the days when I was younger, such programs seemed mildly attractive, though not enough to tempt me away from Grand Beach.

Maybe I was discouraged because no one wants me to do those things. But I don't want to do them either. Yet, there is still a sense of opportunities lost in life. Silly!

Paul Murray's poem today says that when the sun chases away the dark and brings light, it also drives off our fears in the dark, and three parallel stars ignite within us: passion, wakefulness, and joy.

All I experience is a reluctance to get up!

And displeasure with those whose noise wakes me—like today!

And dread at the pressures of the day!

Something is wrong with that, isn't there?

I love You.

March 28, 2001; 8:45 a.m.; Tucson

My Love,

I reflect that in the last week I have been accused of leaving the priesthood, approving abortion, and wanting to change the eucharistic teaching. Also, I have been dismissed as a millionaire. If I am an outsider in the Church, the reason is in substantial part because of lies like that.

My sadness of the past few days (again!) about a wasted life would be much more appropriate if it was sadness about envy that has caused my work to be dismissed by the clerical elite. There is, however, nothing I can do about it, is there? Your Son, an infinitely better person than I, had to put up with similar envy. Those that attack me won't crucify me, though they hate me enough to want to kill my work if not me. Well, that's their problem, not mine!

I love You.

March 30, 2001; 8:40 a.m.; Tucson

My Love,

This is a wonderful morning: blue sky, soft wind, warmth, and no reason to rush. After the last three days, the details of which You know already and I won't bore You with, I can relax when I eat breakfast, start to work in a leisurely fashion, and enjoy my Arizona sojourn as I rarely have this year. It is my fault that there have not been more such days—and that there will be practically none when I return to Chicago.

I could make the case that I've worked hard for forty-seven years in the priesthood and am entitled to slow down a little. You could make a case, probably stronger, that I should have slowed down long ago, indeed that I should never have begun to work at my present pace.

Mostly too late to change, I'm afraid. But I will try.

I saw the movie about Stalingrad the other night. Most accurate war movie (as far as I can tell) yet. So horrible that it looked like science fiction. Protect us from those horrors, I beg You.

And I love You, I really do.

April 1, 2001; 9:05 a.m.; Tucson
My Love,

April Fool's Day and I'm sad. Why?

Because the time in Tucson comes to an end and I've wasted so much of it.

Because the time during April and May in Chicago will be rushed.

Because I don't know whether I'll ever come back.

Because all things go badly.

Because so much of work seems a waste.

Because, unlike the young swans of whom Paul Murray talks in today's poems, I do not lean far out into the wind.

Because I am tired.

Because . . .

Anyway, I love You.

April 2, 2001; 8:50 a.m.; Tucson
My Love,

We all sing from a wound! So Paul Murray tells me in the poem I read today. The wound, if I understand him properly, is the wound of our mortality, the knowledge that we will die. We sing because we will die, in hope of protecting ourselves from sadness, or in hope of defying sadness. We sing because we die and because we hope we will live. That's why we sing!

You may well say that I don't sing at all. Which is true—and your fault, one way or another. I wish I could sing, but that's irrelevant.

Yeats, I find, was tone deaf, yet he heard the music.

I am not Yeats or a Yeats. But I try to sing in my stories. Sing a song of sixpence, pocket full of rye . . . I forget what that means. Sing a song of hope and a song of love. Well, I try.

And I love You.

April 3, 2001; 8:10 a.m.; Tucson
My Love,

Paul Murray writes this morning about how the sound of a bird's call at the end of the day breaks through the diversity of our paths and attunes us to "even the smallest silence."

I heard that bird call yesterday—and even the silence. Not for long because my mind was racing with the story I'm presently writing—as it raced all last night and still races—and the moments of peace were strangled. There is no way, I fear, that I can break away from the story when I'm fully engaged as I am now—though this one, perhaps because of the month when I was unable to work on it, is especially demanding. I shall try again tonight to listen for the bird's song.

I love You.

April 4, 2001; 7:55 a.m.; Tucson

My Love,

Last week in Tucson. Phones ringing, doorbells ringing. People from New York calling at 7:30. And I'm trying to write a novel. I wish I could afford the luxury of turning off the world when I'm writing a story. I can't because of all the other demands in my life. Well, I don't have a wife and a family, so I suppose it evens out. The day has just started and I'm already twitching!

How many times have I made this complaint?

Writing, as I told You yesterday, has somehow become more compelling, more demanding, more enervating. At the end of the day, I am utterly drained. I'm so worn that I can't find You, even in the sounds and sights of the desert. You are, as Paul Murray says in today's poem, "close yet indistinct / like the curve of a face only our / fingers can trace in the dark."

What a beautiful image. Trouble with me these days is that I don't even feel the curve. But I know You're there.

And I still love You.

April 5, 2001; 8:20 a.m.; Tucson

My Love,

Paul Murray puts it well again today: when we try to pray or to feed our minds on your presence, "our thoughts are like words in a dream, our prayers like crumbs falling from the hand of sleep." What a wonderful image, and how painfully true.

I try to pray, even in the situation out here where the conditions are the best of any of my situations. Sometimes, I know You're present and I reach for You. You don't go away, but I do—my mind filled with ideas and images and plans and work, especially at times like the present when I'm working on a story. I keep trying and I get nowhere, yet I believe that You are present in Love and that I can reach You and that You are content with my pathetic efforts.

So I love You and will keep trying, and I pray for all those who today need my prayers.

April 8, 2001 (Palm Sunday); 9:40 a.m.; Tucson

My Love,

A lovely Sunday morning here, music in the background, blue sky, no wind—a day to be enjoyed. So I will work, pack my clothes, finish the novel, write a column. What a fool I am.

I love You.

April 10, 2001; 8:35 a.m.; Tucson

My Love,

Last full day in Tucson. Cold. Rain. All my farewells said. Finishing the novel, maybe today. Sad to leave. Dread what I face in Chicago for the next six weeks.

Thank You for the grace of this place in the sun. So much beauty now that the desert is in bloom. I didn't appreciate it much. Sorry.

Sorry, sorry, sorry.

Wasted life, I tell myself. At least spiritual waste. Forgive.

I know that You love me.

Help me to love You more.

April 13, 2001 (Good Friday); 7:40 a.m.; Chicago

My Love,

I was forced by the disasters of yesterday and this morning (of which You are aware) to do the intelligent, that is the virtuous, thing today: came back after getting a new tire to sleep for two hours. I'm still tired, which shows the extent of my sleep deprivation this week.

It's been one of those times when the story takes over my life and prevents me from thinking or doing anything else. Well, no, that's not true. I do lots of other things, but I'm only half conscious of the world around me, and I exhaust myself. Maybe that's the only way to write a story.

A friend of mine is dying. A few weeks ago he felt fine, in the pink, with perfect health for a man his age. Then his hip started to hurt. They did scans and found cancer in his kidney and his hip. They operated—taking out a rib and a kidney. Now there's rehab. Then a hip replacement, then chemo. Slowly but surely the doctors are dismantling him. Soon there will be nothing left. His wife and kids will go through agonies and then grief after his death.

We are (usually) born healthy, grow for a couple of decades, and then begin to deteriorate . . . we start to die. Dying is a much longer process now than it used be, but the results are the same, are they not? Just as the body of your Son was dismantled by the Romans, so are we all doomed to this dismantling. If today's festival has any meaning, it is that You've been there, done that, know what it's like, and will be with us at the end.

I'm counting on that.

I must live with that truth, not only when death is upon me, but in the little hints of it that are part of daily life.

I love You, especially on this day when your love for us was never more manifest.

April 14, 2001 (Holy Saturday); 7:00 a.m.; Chicago
My Love,

The city is quiet this morning, perhaps no more quiet than it is on other Saturday mornings.

I continue to be dull and senseless. Still recovering from return. Off to NY next week, silly venture.

Some absolute nightmare schedule for the next six weeks, not all my fault. Things don't work.

The secret these next weeks is to survive.

I love You.

April 15, 2001 (Easter Sunday); 8:30 p.m.; Chicago
My Love,

Why is it that on holidays I spend most of my time in the car? It has always been that way, as far as I can remember. At the end of the day I come back to my room tired—weary, discouraged, depressed, grim.

I don't know, or I guess I do know. It's not your fault, but my fault—or maybe it is your fault for making me the kind of person I am.

This is the feast of your Resurrection, a time for the celebration of new life. I'm too worn out to celebrate anything. So I have to yield myself to You in exhaustion, knowing that this is not the way to celebrate the Christian Passover—but this is, in the circumstances, what I must do. And if I'm tired, You love me just the same.

Anyway I love You. Thank You for the gift of life and of new life.

April 16, 2001; 1:30 p.m.; Chicago
My Love,

1:30: I've been rushing all morning. Not a chance to get to prayer till now.

One of the reasons I am always discouraged is the constant abuse, particularly from priests, but also from Catholic laity, right and left. There is obviously something about me that stirs up deep anger. Also in sociologists and book reviewers.

I know the reasons for the hate and the anger—and the pretense that I do not exist. I know that they are the same reasons that sent your Son to his death. I know they go with the territory. Yet, they're not true, I hear myself saying. Of course they're not true—like the right-wing rumor that I have been suspended. I have not reacted well to all of this stuff. It's like they have vomited on me.

After all these years I should know how to react. At least I don't fire e-mails back to them. Still, I let them deprive me of the peace and happiness I should have, and that's a mistake.

Help me to laugh at them, and prevent my fantasies about getting even.
I love You.

April 21, 2001; 8:35 a.m.; Chicago

My Love,

Back from New York. Rough time. Tired—again. Opera, plays, museums were wonderful. TV interviews abominable.

Need time to rest.
I love You.

April 22, 2001; 9:05 a.m.; Chicago

My Love,

Gloomy April Sunday, rain pouring down. Fits my mood. I feel battered by the attacks of recent weeks and especially by what was supposed to be a friendly TV interview, one that I was doing as a "favor for a friend." Never again for that bunch!

I face the fact that my public image, what most people think I am, is accurately reflected by the interview—a bishop attacking, sex-obsessed priest. The people who read my novels know better, as do those who know my work. However, the myth is strong, unbreakable.

Words from Paul Murray seem appropriate this morning: "never again to lust / after dreams / or to allow / the hurt of the past / to unhinge / the real world."

I find myself wondering this morning what is the real world.
Anyway, I love You.

April 24, 2001; 8:45 a.m.; Chicago

My Love,

Still tired and discouraged.

I've been reading a travel book about the Christian remnants in the Middle East—Armenians, Greeks, Surians, Nestorians, various kinds of Christian Arabs—and how, after a millennium and a half, they are finally being driven out by the Turks and the Iranians and the Palestinians and the Fundamental-ists and the Israelis. So much terror, rape, and murder, past and present.

And the Maronite Catholics are every bit as bad.

How can You tolerate such stuff? I understand that You wipe away every tear, but I still can't figure it out. I know I'm not supposed to.

Or the missionary and her baby daughter shot down by a Peruvian jet with help from the CIA. How can these things be? How can any suffering be—or all suffering?

I know I'm not supposed to figure it out. I hope You have. It has to be better someplace.

I told You I was in a bad mood.

Jack Durkin's anniversary Mass tonight. How we miss him!

I love You.

April 25, 2001; 8:15 a.m.; Chicago

My Love,

We had the seventh anniversary Mass last night for Jack Durkin, a proper Catholic celebration and remembrance, though his loss still leaves and will always leave a gaping hole in our family. Also, my sister Grace is in a bad way again, slowly starving herself to death. Mary Jule and I think it is now legitimate to ask You if You will please call her home and grant her a life, one that, for some reason or the other, she never had here. Thy will be done.

These two brushes with death in the family do not greatly contribute to pulling me out of my long-term weariness and discouragement. It would be easier, I think, if I were not doing as much work as I always have. But how to stop.

Help me, please, to know what to do and what not to do. Perhaps I'm making a little progress.

I love You.

April 26, 2001; 7:35 a.m.; Chicago

My Love,

My Easter lilies are dead. So quickly has Easter come and gone that I hardly noticed. Every once in a while I find myself thinking that Easter is still to come, though I am writing homilies for the Seventh Week of Easter. Everything comes and goes so quickly. And each morning I'm awake and at this computer grinding out stuff: e-mail, columns, homilies, articles, papers, novels, sociology books.

Why?

Because I like to, because I have no choice, because I think You want me to, though perhaps not so much, because it all helps some people. I would like to be able to stop. At least I think I would. Maybe if I stopped I'd be miserably unhappy. Maybe it's a sterile life, though I don't think so.

I don't know. I don't know about anything.

Except that I try to love You.

April 27, 2001; 4:05 p.m.; Chicago

My Love,

A gorgeous spring day—turquoise lake, blessed-mother blue sky, red and gold tulips blooming outside NORC, trees budding. Just busting out all over. So I came back from NORC and have sat at this machine all day working on the millennium book, an article about George Higgins, and an article on liturgists.

Well, I did look out of the window a lot and smile at the city in springtime.

Thank You for all the beauty. I'm coming down the home stretch on my work, but how many times have I said that? I will have everything done, I think, by the end of the weekend, except the bibliography for the book and an article on the parish as social capital.

How many times since ordination have I thought I was about to clear up all the work and I've never done so?

I wondered as I was reading *From the Holy Mount* whether I should perhaps choose the monastic life as a way to end my life. There is something to be said for peace and simplicity. It has an appeal, but it would probably be false to my vocation. I can't quit now, can I?

Or should I?

My instincts—what else to use when dealing with You?—say that I should die as I live: busy, active, and a little manic. Help me.

I love You.

April 28, 2001; 9:20 a.m.; Chicago

My Love,

The city seems quiet this Saturday morning: only a few cars on the avenue, the expressway open, a scattering of people on the streets, cranes motionless, no wind. I listen more closely and I hear construction sounds, a car horn, a plane. The el tracks empty. The city is gray today with a few splashes of light blue and red and white. All dreary and lifeless, or maybe it's me that's dreary and lifeless. So much anger piled up through the years. Not good.

I love You.

May 2, 2001; 8:15 a.m.; Chicago

My Love,

Several days of no prayer and no swimming. I've been moving in a fog of discouragement and sleep deprivation. My own fault, partially. I tried to do much and, more than that, I let the *murmurantes* get to me. Also, external forces interfered with my sleep. Last night I had a good night and feel wonderful this morning, for which many thanks.

Spring is glorious. All the flowering trees. Why do they not flower all summer long? Do they in heaven? I hope so.

Grand Beach next week for a few days—some of those days hopefully on retreat.

Thank You for bringing me back to earth—perhaps I should say back up to earth from the caves of despond.

I love You.

May 3, 2001; 9:25 a.m.; Chicago

My Love,

Are You a dream, You strangely tolerant and passionately loving person to whom I pore out my complaints and my fears and my hopes every morning? It would be interesting if someone went through these reflections and analyzed the nature of the one to whom I think I'm talking, like You were a character in one of my novels, which come to think of it, maybe You are—a creation of my own imagination of the kind of God I would like to have or that I need. Am I talking to myself?

In a way I am. I can imagine You only in terms of my own experience of lesser persons, and thus think of You as a combination of the best traits of the best people I know. I have created You not so much in my own image and likeness as in the image and likeness of people I think reflect You.

What else can I do?

However, as Paul Murray says in the poem I read this morning, if You are part of *my* dreams, then I believe that I am part of *your* dreams, too. Why You would bother dreaming about someone like me, I have no idea. But You do because You love me.

The best I can do is to reply that I love You.

May 4, 2001; 8:25 a.m.; Chicago

My Love,

I'm ashamed of myself this morning. I didn't help someone yesterday who needed help and had called on me. I should have realized what the call meant, but I didn't, perhaps because I was busy with other things, perhaps because I didn't want to, and perhaps because the other person annoys me. I am sorry. I will find a way to make it up to the other with your help.

I do not like the person I am these weeks, as people close in on me from all sides, filling up my calendar, preventing both work and relaxation. Nor do I like how the work in which I am engaged obsesses me. This is a bad time. I shouldn't be pushing myself the way I do. I shouldn't let my swim slip away at the end of the day. I shouldn't be rushing all the time.

I look forward to my time at Grand Beach when all this is swept away.

But I know that it will never be.

Help me.

I'm sorry.

I love You.

May 5, 2001; 9:40 a.m.; Chicago

My Love,

Cinco de mayo—forty-seventh anniversary of ordination. A cold day like it was in 1954, though cloudy and rainy today.

I have no inclination to celebrate it. I gave up on celebrations long ago, and endure them for the sake of others.

I am happy to be a priest and happy to have survived so long in the priesthood. However . . .

However what?

However, I find clerical culture so oppressive that I do not even want to go to the celebration next week. I will of course.

I wonder if there is no celebration energy left in me, no enjoyment energy, no sense of accomplishment? Am I running, so to speak, on automatic pilot? Have the *murmurantes* finally caught up with me? If they have, the reason is that I've let them. I'm sorry.

Anyway, I am very grateful for my priestly vocation and for the long years in the priesthood and for all the priests and laity who have influenced me.

And I regret the sadness which has taken over my life.

I love You, just the same.

May 6, 2001; 5:55 p.m.; Grand Beach

My Love,

It's great to be back here. I collapsed into bed this afternoon and slept for two hours, showing how much sleep deprivation I have piled up. Already I feel relaxed, even though the place is a mess, as it usually is this time of the year. The sadness lingers.

I love You.

May 7, 2001; 8:00 a.m.; Grand Beach

My Love,

How quickly and easily I relax up here. It doesn't last, but it's what this place should be about. I saw again *Diary of a Country Priest* last night. It reminds me of my first days in the parish. Unlike the cure, I was smart, articulate, energetic, and gave the impression I knew what I was doing— which offended many people in the parish, as he offended his. Unlike him, I didn't have stomach cancer and am not a saint.

Yet, I believe what he did about You and about others. You love them all— and I must love them, too.

I feel so much of a failure as a priest, despite all my presumed successes. And he was a success, despite all his apparent failures.

Is that a fair picture of me and my ministry? I think not, but that is a part of my sadness as my life winds down.

I'm sorry that I've missed so many opportunities.
I love You.

May 8, 2001; 8:45 a.m.; Grand Beach
My Love,

Priesthood all around me. Sunday *Diary of a Country Priest*, yesterday *Murder in Holy Orders*, tonight *M. Vincent*. All forcing me to question not so much my vocation as how I have responded to my vocation as I approach the communal celebration of our ordination on Thursday.

I cannot escape the feeling that I have failed. I am not prayerful enough, not patient enough, not restrained enough in my anger; too busy about too many things and too subject to bitterness over my rejection. I now take the rejection for granted (though there's plenty of acceptance, too), but I am still bitter and often angry over it.

When I try to articulate the reasons for my sadness, some of it is . . . is what? I don't know! It just is.

Maybe I haven't lived up to the ideal of forty-seven years ago. I've tried but I haven't even come close. Yet, I have worked hard, and not really to promote my name, though perhaps too much to defend myself.

Still confused? I guess so.

Well, at least I've tried.

I love You.

May 9, 2001; 7:30 a.m.; Grand Beach
My Love,

I'm troubled this morning. You know why, and I don't want to mention it explicitly. I'm caught up in conflicting emotions and have a hard time straightening out my reactions. Help me to know what to do. In these matters, I generally follow my instincts; what else is there to follow?

I watched *M. Vincent* last night. A great film and a great critique of priesthood, my priesthood, which is all I should be concerned about. Again, I've followed my instincts as to what your Holy Spirit wants me to do, but I am painfully aware of the risks of self-deception.

Why do I write my novels? First of all, I have always said—and I believe it—that I write to retell stories of grace, of your forgiving love. Secondly, because I enjoy writing. How does lifestyle and fame figure in? I don't do it for the money, though the money is useful. However, my lifestyle has changed only marginally.

Having thus examined my conscience, I am still uneasy, which arguably is a good way for me to be.

I love You.

May 12, 2001; 9:15 a.m.; Chicago

My Love,

The anniversary gathering was sad. So much pain, so much suffering, so much disillusionment, so much disappointment. By comparison, my difficulties have been minor. We were all so young and so happy and so ambitious and so confident. That's all over now, and we're holding on and clinging to life and to memories, not all of which are good.

I have my work still, and all the stuff I do. While it wears me out, it at least keeps me vital, and I'm grateful for that.

I pray for all of these men with whom we were together on St. Crispin's Day. Take care of them and protect them. While we may have little in common anymore, we spent our youth together in terrible conditions.

And whatever else, we're still priests.

Before I came in from Grand Beach, I saw three French films about priests: *Diary*, *M. Vincent*, and *Leo Morin, Priest*. All three were good priests in the old mode. The priesthood then was a respected group, even in France. Now we have men leaving en masse, pedophiles, sexually active priests. The image has slipped. Not that any of these things didn't happen before, but it's now all public. The leadership has not handled these problems well, at all, at all.

Bad stuff.

Nonetheless, I'm glad I'm still a priest—and that I became one.

I'm a happy priest.

Thank You.

I love You.

May 13, 2001; 8:25 a.m.; Chicago

My Love,

Mother's Day. Thank You for my mother, who had such a great influence on me in ways I don't understand but were extremely important for my development. Her life was not a happy one, save perhaps for a few years. I'm so sorry about that, not that there was anything I could do.

I pray, too, for all the mothers in the world who give so much and get so little back. I think of all the mothers at OSP this morning who were clutching their kids—so much love and so much conflict ahead. Terrible.

I visited my sister in the nursing home this morning after hearing my younger sister preach at OSP. A most unsatisfactory interlude.

What can I do?

I love You. Help me to love You more.

May 14, 2001; 8:35 a.m.; Chicago

My Love,

In the poem I read this morning, Paul Murray tells of the sun rising at the end of a difficult night. "I have come through / after all. I have a new / dawn on my shoulders."

A new dawn and a new week, new promises, new prospects, new challenges, new chances. Life goes on, however rapidly and erratically. I draw together my battered fragments and keep trying. Please help me on the way. Grant that I may be charming and thus reflect your love.

I love You.

May 15, 2001; 8:10 a.m.; Chicago

My Love,

I wake up this morning to a nice apartment, papers delivered to my door, classical music on the radio, the prospect of an interesting day, apparent good health, the Grand Beach summer stretching out ahead of me, an exciting if exhausting life . . . I am not grateful enough.

My complaint, should I dare to make one, is that my work is ignored. That is perhaps my own fault for being a dissident (of a sort). However, I have, I think, followed the Spirit, and if that is the result, it is not one that ought to concern me all that much.

So this morning, I thank You for the incredibly good things in my life, and I ask that I be more aware of your constant goodness to me.

I love You.

May 16, 2001; 7:55 a.m.; Chicago

My Love,

Our early summer continues—90 degrees yesterday. Very nice, thank You, just so long as it doesn't rain all through July!

I continue to be very busy, lunch and supper every day. Yesterday's lunch was interesting. A young woman who had just passed her Ph.D. exam in English (on Hemingway), who had been reading my novels since she was in high school because her parents had passed them on to her. They have played an important part in her life. She understood them, as did her parents.

So I have accomplished something, even if I'm a permanent outsider around here—which, as I have often said, is my own fault.

Her appreciation of the stories was wonderful. Thank You much for that grace. I know there are tens of thousands like her out there. I should take heart and believe in what I'm doing.

I love You.

May 17, 2001; 9:46 a.m.; Chicago

My Love,

The poems I read in *Poetry* are blasphemous. They attack You directly for not protecting humans from suffering, which proves You don't really exist and are not much better than the Aztec god who devoured the bodies of young men and women. As if the vagaries of life are under your direct control, and as if your promise of life superabundant doesn't apply only in the long run.

One poet laments that his life, so precious to him, will quickly be forgotten. He has done nothing memorable.

The temptation to that kind of despair is seductive, especially on a gray morning when rain threatens. Life is nothing—empty, meaningless, an exercise in self-deception. Why bother with anything? There is a school of thought that says we should be grateful for life even if it is pointless.

I reject all that stuff. I believe in You and your love, though I don't understand You—and never will. My life is a little less pointless because of my books. Yet, they will be forgotten, as even now they are ignored.

Life is too short. But your love lasts forever and I cling to that.

I love You.

May 20, 2001; 7:35 a.m.; Chicago

My Love,

Melancholy weekend—Jack Egan died yesterday, and there was a farewell for John Piderit, who is leaving Loyola this morning. My talk at the synagogue in between went well enough.

I pray for both of those good men. Egan was eighty-six, and one of the great priests of the diocese. The cardinal wept when he heard of his death. I'm grateful that we straightened out our relationship through your grace. Take care of them both for me, if You would.

I love You.

May 22, 2001; 9:30 a.m.; Chicago

My Love,

Still pondering Jack Egan's life and death. I owe him a lot. I regret the conflicts that arose between us. There were times I was dubious about his enthusiasms, times when I felt he had let me down. For those reactions, I am sorry, insofar as they caused me to forget that he was a man with a great heart. I am so glad that I reconciled with him years ago. I must continue to try to reconcile with people and to forgive, even though my memory still haunts me with a sense of betrayal. Yet, I must be a difficult friend, at least for some people.

I am straightening out my apartment and throwing stuff out. Many memories there, too—some good, some terrible. Again, I often reacted badly, which is not to say that others didn't, too. I've never quite come to terms with the fact that so many people dislike me, even if they've never met me.

Yet, some have met me and they dislike me even more. However, a lot of people like me, too. I guess You have made me that kind of person.

I am sorry today for all the goofy things I've done under pressure.

While we were having lunch, a sparrow crashed into the big windows of the yacht club and died, poor thing. He did not fall without You knowing about it and feeling sorry for the poor thing. How can You cope with all that?

The *Times* had a long article in its science section today about "pre-creation," about eternity before it was time. Headache material. What were You doing, the article wondered (without too much irreverence), when there was nothing to do anything with? I don't know. It's not important that I know. It's important that I believe in your love and try to reply each day as best I can.

I love You.

May 23, 2001; 8:20 a.m.; Chicago
My Love,

I read this morning an essay in *Poetry* by a poet who is caught between the need for meaning and the demands that modernity imposes that there can be no meaning. There has to be meaning. We humans cannot accept the conclusion that death is the end. Hence, even in Europe the number of atheists is small, and most believe somehow in life after death. Meaning survives, even after a century of modernity.

I think of the terrible grief of those who have lost their loves, even those whose faith tells them that it is not the end of their love. Is life eventually only tragic, or is there more?

I believe in more, though sometimes it is difficult. But then it is not supposed to be easy. I agree with W. James that it is unthinkable that we not see our loves again. Help my faith. Give me greater clarity about my life.

I love You.

May 28, 2001; 8:10 a.m.; Grand Beach
My Love,

Five cold and rainy days here at Grand Beach. That's the way Memorial Day is, however.

Lots of thoughts about the people killed in wars and the people left behind. The usual question is why You permit such things. The only appropriate answer is that You can't stop them.

Why not? Ah, that's the mystery, isn't it?

I love this place so much because it means not a peaceful quiet life, but one that is *more* peaceful and quiet than Chicago life. The next eight days are going to be difficult. I must try to be cheerful at the meeting in Sweden, even though I'll be jet-lagged, and the midnight sun seems likely to be obscured by four days of rain!

It is raining everywhere!

People tell me I look much more relaxed than I have in previous summers. That is surely true for which, many thanks.

And for my Grand Beach refuge, too.

I love You.

May 30, 2001; 8:00 a.m.; Chicago

My Love,

At GB I read a novel by Jean Sulivan, a French priest. He is very good and very French, which is his privilege. It's about a priest who worked in the Pigalle district of Paris with prostitutes, obviously a saint if an unorthodox one. Sulivan emphasizes the "freedom" of Strozzi, as the priest is called. He is not bound by rules and by structures, but only by faith and love.

This is a theme that recurs frequently in French novels and suggests how rigid the structures of church and state are in France. No glancing back over the shoulder to see what authorities, civil or religious, might be following him. Without realizing it, I developed that theme in *The Bishop and the Beggar Girl.* The government and the church in this country would not have closed in on Frere Jean Claude the way the French did.

Yet, Sulivan's point is still well-taken, even in our society and our church. I have been "put in a box," as someone has said, by my archdiocese and by the clergy, and that has given me a lot of freedom. I will willingly pay the price, but it wasn't freedom I sought.

Or was it? Certainly during my days at CK I wanted more freedom, though not necessarily this much.

Should I compare myself to Strozzi? Why not? We should always compare ourselves to saints. I should be more generous.

Yet, I refused to go on CNN last night to talk about this African archbishop who married a Moonie. Not generous?

Hardly. The free person is also free to keep his mouth shut.

Anyway, protect me on this trip to New Orleans. I am uneasy about the reaction.

I love You.

June 10, 2001; 8:40 a.m.; Grand Beach

My Love,

Back from Sweden, down here at last, trying to get things lined up. Beginning to relax finally.

No reflection for the last ten days. Sorry. Very gloomy some of the time. Bad dreams. (Last night I blew off Fidel Castro's head in a dream, but only because he was about to kill me!)

Midnight sun was very nice. Meeting was good, but only because I took a nap after breakfast and after lunch.

The gloominess is connected with death and with the feeling that I've wasted my life, which maybe I have, but it was not from want of good intent. I must truly relax and refresh this summer. Help me, please.

I love You.

June 11, 2001; 8:40 a.m.; Grand Beach
My Love,

I've been reading Bob McGovern's poems. They are quite good, easily accessible (which kind of violates the rules of poetry), very Catholic, filled with love and faith and dense with irony, the kind of irony that comes with age and a consciousness of human suffering and death.

How does one live with, understand, and transcend this irony? He does, though obviously with a struggle. One cannot do it without a struggle.

I look back on my life and think "failure." Obviously I have not failed at everything, just those things I thought to be important. The success of the novels doesn't cancel out the failures, and even they are not all that successful.

So I think at the beginning of the Grand Beach season. Perhaps this summer, as I write and reflect and renew, I will see more clearly.

I love You.

June 12, 2001; 9:50 a.m.; Grand Beach
My Love,

In one of McG's poems I read about a priest—brother, maybe, or uncle—who could not accept the council and, in the name of the pope, rejected the pope. There were some like that, not a lot. Michael Cuneo described them in his book: pathetic men mostly, defending the true faith against an ecumenical council approved by the pope. More recently, they, and some of the rich laity, have been rejuvenated by the present pope and the Curia.

It is a strange time, and has been for the last couple of decades, a time of disappointments, frustrations, confusions, almost as though the Church has not been able to make up its mind.

The figures I dug up over the weekend about contributions show the strain. People are still loyal to the Church (albeit on their own terms), but the joy seems to have gone out of it. They're angry and no one in authority believes they're angry.

Anyway, like I say, I've flourished. I regret that the Church has not.

I love You.

June 13, 2001; 7:35 a.m.; Grand Beach
My Love,

I went down to both marinas yesterday to see to the boats for the summer. There is a strong air of excitement, expectation in these milieux: summer has come, boats are in the lake or going in, good times are ahead. Above all, SUMMER!

Touches of that still affect me, even though sailing and waterskiing may be a little much for me these days.

SUMMER is wonderful; each precious day must be treasured, but not compulsively, not as something to cling to desperately, as do those who have no hope.

Deepen and enrich my hope. I believe, I love, I hope!

Maybe it's the other way around. Hope comes first, then belief, then love. So today, I say simply I hope.

And that I love You.

June 14, 2001; 9:20 a.m.; Grand Beach
My Love,

It's been such a long time since 1968—and yet it seems only yesterday . . . so I thought when I watched the segment from *Hair* the other night at the Dunes Theatre. I sat out that era, neither protesting nor marching, merely watching in dismay from up here as we let some of our young people tear our society apart—and then saw them, filled with self-pity, as they "sold out." As if they had ever not been what they were: the indulged and the self-indulged. And now they're the Bobos.

They created Nixon and Reagan and the present incumbent. Big deal!

I'm thinking of that again this morning, because Bob McGovern's poems from that era call back both the desperation and the folly. It seems that I've been losing ever since.

Which is one of the dumbest things I've ever said.

I still struggle for meaning in my foolish life, as though it's not there every morning in my e-mail.

Why do I let the *mumurantes* bother me? I don't know. I haven't figured out the trajectories.

Yet, I love You—and I hope.

June 15, 2001; 7:40 a.m.; Grand Beach
My Love,

Yesterday I read the story of the rescue of survivors of the Bataan Death March by a group of Rangers during the invasion of Luzon in 1945. Brave men both. The horrors of Japanese culture were portrayed dispassionately: the torture and murder of prisoners (whom the Japanese delighted in beheading with their big swords), the suicidal charges. When in trouble, one Filipino guerrilla leader said, they abandon tactics and simply charge into certain death. On the other hand, there was the horror of the death of the Japanese in the surprise attack of the Rangers on the troops temporarily quartered at the camp. One minute alive and chatting, the next moment dead.

Not a culture to be trusted much.

But the horror of war for both the killers and the killed. Dear God, how terrible! So many lives cut short, so many widows and orphans, so much suffering. Evil, evil, evil. One prays that it will never happen again. One knows it will.

Protect us all, I beg You.

I love You. I try to hope.

June 16, 2001; 9:00 a.m.; Grand Beach

My Love,

I am very angry, as You know well. Moreover, I have reason to be angry. Still, I must calm down and deal with the cause—only after I'm calmed down. Please help me.

I love You.

June 18, 2001; 7:00 a.m.; Grand Beach

My Love,

I did calm down and, with your help, handled the problem skillfully. Thank You.

Seamus Heaney has an interesting metaphor in one of his poems: "I feel like a soul being prayed for." What does that feel like? I'm not sure, but it's still a line-stopping metaphor.

Do I ever feel that way? Not much. Rather, I feel like a soul being cursed, hated, damned by so many people; a soul ignored; a soul put in the box. Why do I feel that way? At least some of the e-mail writers offer their prayers for me, which is very nice, but I doubt that's typical.

Well, do You pray for me? What need do you have to pray for anyone? You're God, the one to whom we all pray. Parents, of course, pray for their children. You're a parent. Ergo?

At least You have the same love for me as a parent does, so the same impulse that leads to parental prayer. So that is reassuring. You care about me positively, even if so many others want to put me in the box. That should be enough. So I hope.

And I love You.

June 19, 2001; 8:10 a.m.; Grand Beach
My Love,

Didn't sleep much last night. Day of struggle with data. Bad. Spring almost over. Summer looming after a sunrise or two. St. John's night. I must get my life in order.

I love You!

June 20, 2001; 9:30 a.m.; Grand Beach
My Love,

Another terrible night last night. This has to stop. Probably too much rich food. Also more interpersonal tension. This has to stop, too. More direct talk.

Too much time wasted on afternoon nap. Too long, but I needed it.

Garden about to erupt in color. Thank You.

Longest day of the year. Thank You for that.

Thank You for summer at long last come.

I hope. I love.

I love You.

June 21, 2001; 8:55 a.m.; Grand Beach
My Love,

First day of summer, longest day of the year, rain and cold. Had to turn the heat on. Very funny!

I should, however, finish most of my work before the day is over, for which I will be very grateful.

Then to the poetry and reflection, like I say every summer.

I love You.

June 25, 2001; 9:05 a.m.; Grand Beach
My Love,

Bad news this morning: Jack Hotchkin died recently. Grant him please the rest and peace and joy that his restless spirit always craved. So much waste . . . But what do I know!

I find myself asking if I could have done anything. Surely not. Could I have done more? Maybe, who knows? Still, I grieve for him, lament his passing, mourn the sadness of his life.

Also troubling information about Marilyn and Brigid Goggin. My heart is heavy with worry and anxiety. Take care of them, I beg You.

Not my will but thine be done.

I love You.

June 26, 2001; 8:10 a.m.; Grand Beach
My Love,

Many sad thoughts about H yesterday and today. I knew him better, I think, than anyone, and yet I didn't know him at all. I reflected on all the incidents in our years, on how much fun we had, and how odd he was at times. I examine the decisions I made, and would make them all again, though with less confidence perhaps. I would have tried to stay in touch with him more than I did, and I regret that. I would not have been able to change anything, but at least he would have known I cared about him. Our occasional meetings in D.C., when I was there and had time, were not much. Yet, how much more would have been too much?

I will look forward to working this out with him later on.

He died in his room at the staff house, heart attack I guess. No previous heart trouble. A good way to go. Maybe.

There's a touch of mystery about it. No point in wondering.

Take good care of him, I beg You.

I hope we will meet again—and I love You.

June 27, 2001; 7:40 p.m.; Grand Beach
My Love,

I'm a strange one, as You well know.

I began my poetry writing today. Another poem about the Moon. A happy joyous poem, I guess. But I personally am neither happy nor joyous. Too many things went wrong this week. I am weary of the battles, tempted to give it all up, tempted to wonder why I hang on.

Silly temptation. It comes every summer at this time when I wind down. I must listen to the poet rather than the pessimist. The poet is a comic.

I love You.

June 28, 2001; 8:00 a.m. Grand Beach
My Love,

My morale is better today than it was last night. I still can't quite figure out why one part of me can write giddy poetry and another part lets itself be weighted down by sadness. The word is well chosen to convey my feelings, *sadness* about so many failures, disappointments, discouragements, rejections. So much effort, so little accomplished.

I must recapture the joy of the past, which is still inside me and which, with your help, has survived.

Sleep helps!

I love You.

July 1, 2001; 8:40 a.m.; Grand Beach
My Love,

Coldest July 1 in history! Well, recorded history.

Autumn already?

Anyway, the days earlier this week were wonderful, "perfect, shimmering summer days" as your man Seamus describes them.

I wanted to hug them, cling to them, never let them go. They were so perfect. You were in them. Of course, that can't be done. We must be ready to let them go. But thanks for the days; they were wonderful.

I love You.

July 4, 2001 (Independence Day); 8:15 a.m.; Grand Beach
My Love,

Thank You for the independence of this country, the best in the world for all its faults.

Thank You for the celebrations, too, which last night down on the beach were sensational.

I had phone conversation with Joe Bernardin last night, which was unusual because only after the conversation did I realize he was dead! A dream, of course, though very realistic. He was trying to tell me about something that he had not been able to say when he was still alive. It's not clear to me now what it was. The phone connection was broken. I tried to call him back, but either the line was busy or there was no answer.

It's easy to account for the dream because of the Mass at the cathedral earlier in the day and the present conflicts there. I don't take it as a revelation of anything, but rather as an indication of my own anxieties about the Church and the wasted opportunities and the conflict between the present cardinal and, as he admits, his most effective priests.

And also my ambivalence about my own forty-year relationship with Jack. Like I say, perhaps we can straighten all that out later on.

I believe that we all survive and will all be young again.

And I love You.

July 7, 2001; 8:35 a.m.; Grand Beach
My Love,

Another glorious summer day, which I want to embrace and cling to and never let go of. That's all I can think of these days, the wonderful and ephemeral summer day. Is its wonder or its transience more revelatory? I vote for wonder, as You know, but with the usual hesitation and doubts.

We saw *A.I.* last night. Too long. Spielberg couldn't figure out how to end it. Still compelling. Profoundly religious, if ambiguously so. Neither he nor Kubrick is sure that life has any meaning at all.

A reasonable position.

Not mine, however.

I cling to mine sometimes by my fingertips. On the other hand, as always, the beauty of this day has to reveal other, richer, deeper, and eternal beauty—which I love as best I can.

I love You.

July 9, 2001; 7:10 a.m.; Grand Beach

My Love,

A good weekend working with Mike on our book, for which we now begin to see daylight at the end of the tunnel. Many thanks.

The weather continues fine. Also thanks for that.

Can it be July 9 already? Summer will be half over next weekend.

Not fair!

I love You.

July 11, 2001; 9:40 a.m.; Grand Beach

My Love,

Quiet here this morning, or at least it was till the phone and the fax began to ring. Time to return to the poetry and relaxing on the beach. Also, I slept well last night. Having guests is wonderful, but it's work. I learn why hospitality is a virtue.

Off to Pine Lake now. Perhaps to get out of the water.

I love You.

Later

I did get out of the water for the first time this summer. I have no idea why. Or how I did right what I've been doing wrong. Muscle memory returned, Sean says. I guess so. I am exhilarated (greatly) from the success and from the ride itself. I know You know, but I wanted to tell You and thank You.

I love You.

July 12, 2001; 9:15 a.m.; Grand Beach

My Love,

Today is my mother's birthday. She is all too dim a memory, though her love and example had a big influence on me. She had a hard life, poverty as a child, failing memory and Alzheimer's later in life, diabetes, my father's discouraged silence because of the Depression. Yet, she was a good woman who kept her faith in often trying circumstances. I certainly love her and miss her even today. I look forward to encountering her again as the young woman she was and whom I dimly and happily remember through the fogs of the past. Take good care of her for me.

I love You.

July 16, 2001; 8:05 a.m.; Grand Beach

My Love,

The Bears leave for Platteville today. So summer is half over. Actually it won't be half over for me until next week because I was in Umea for the first week in June.

See how compulsive I am about summer. I love the time up here, the beauty of the garden and the beach and the lake—so much. However, they are lures to a greater beauty that I believe in.

I am reading Dave Toolan's new book, which has some of the best spirituality I have encountered in a long time. I will reread the closing chapters very carefully in the days ahead.

He depicts You as an energy, an overwhelming force that is in all the processes of your creation driving toward a goal of your own which we cannot fully understand, a goal that incurs risk for You because it can only be reached in some fashion with our cooperation.

The energy is of course Love.

It's at work in the glacier that shapes the lake, in the waves that pound rocks into sand on the beach (and at the bottom of the lake), in the cycles that produce the plants and trees, in my work and in my loves, in the workings of our bodies and of every force of nature that shapes the space in which we live. That close?

I believe that, and will try not to be depressed at the end of summer.

Which is still a long way off, isn't it?

I love You.

July 18, 2001; 8:25 a.m.; Grand Beach

My Love,

You, Dave Toolan tells us, are a risk taker, a gambler. There are no safety nets.

I like that metaphor, though I would add that You also love each of us, indeed every creature that You've produced: the bird in the air, the lily in my garden. That's a big order, but since You are in the creation as the driving energy, You must love, since that energy finally is the energy of love.

All that makes me feel very small and very dumb. I can't comprehend what You're up to (if I could, You wouldn't be God). I am a fragile bit of cosmic fluff. Loved, indeed, but still fragile.

Time slips through my fingers as summer does. I am so unimportant. I feel unimportant and, in a certain sense, doomed. I know that I'm not, but that's the way I feel this morning.

Help me.

I love You.

July 19, 2001; 7:55 a.m.; Grand Beach

My Love,

I was sick yesterday, probably too much to eat the day before, but also a fever. I apologize for being a big surly.

The issue finally is whether You are as good as You say You are, whether, for all the risks You take, You still take care of the least of your creatures. You say You do. I wouldn't not believe You. If You are You, then You are able to take care of them eventually—and will do so.

But what about the dinosaurs, so dearly loved by kids today? Well, You take care of them, too, I guess.

But it is a pretty competitive world, isn't it not?

Stories about women with postpartum depression in the paper, like Nuala Anne in *Irish Love*. One drowns her four children. One here in Chicago drowns herself after giving birth to quads. You must love them all and will take care of them eventually. You too give birth and in some way agonize over what happens.

Take care of these women and their children and all like them, as the loving mother that You are.

I love You.

July 20, 2001; 9:40 a.m.; Grand Beach

My Love,

Toolan lists all the names by which You are known in the Jewish scriptures: faithful husband, boxer, warrior, potter, judge, physician, thief, farmer, redeemer, executioner, slave owner, destroyer, hero, archer, savior, consoler, strong arm, teacher, bridegroom, midwife, mother, jealous lover, stranger, seducer, enemy, butcher, guard, and mason. God is also lion, dew, light, tree, stream, bear, stumbling stone, trap, shelter, shade, drought, restaurateur, rock, crown, bird, the sun, fortress, eagle, a mace, shield, stronghold, thunderstorm, lamp, song, wind, cloud, and fire.

That's a pretty impressive list, a story behind each image. How we humans struggle to catch a glimpse of You. We fail, but not for want of trying. Or maybe I should say we do catch all kinds of glimpses but neither individually nor collectively are they enough to satisfy us.

My favorite is not on the list: lover, not jealous lover, but simply lover.

And I try as best as I can in my own stumbling, weary, frequently depressed way to respond to that love.

I love You.

July 21, 2001; 8:15 a.m.; Grand Beach

My Love,

Now summer is officially half over. Thanks for it so far.

Take care, please, of my special intentions.

Swimming last night, there were lights everywhere—airplanes from O'Hare almost indistinguishable from the fireflies. Glorious.

Your servant Augustine wondered about the mosquito. I think that problem has been answered. More serious is the question of why the fireflies. I understand that their lights are part of the evolutionary process and serve for their survival, but they're so wonderful when they dart about on a hot summer night, sparking out little bursts of beauty, little hints of You.

Well done, my Love, very well done!

A priest told me last night how much I had meant to him before and during his priesthood. I was delighted and embarrassed. I could perhaps have helped others if they had given me a chance . . . Anyway, thank You.

And I love You.

July 22, 2001; 8;45 a.m.; Grand Beach

My Love,

I watched a late-afternoon thunderstorm come across the lake, touching the waves gently, blowing the trees lightly, and then becoming fierce. The radar shows a big one heading right at us, but no rain yet. Maybe it will blow over and I'll have to turn on the hose again.

I feel that this weekend and this Sunday have been wasted, though I have done some reading and have written my column and dictated my mail. I feel that the whole summer has been wasted. Maybe because I'm not doing much.

Nutty idea!

I must continue to try to relax and read. Poetry tomorrow for sure.

I love You.

July 23, 2001; 9:45 p.m.; Grand Beach

My Love,

Late in the evening I ask myself if I've wasted another day. Silly notion, but so many of my notions are silly. I played with the photographic stuff on the computer and learned something. Is that a waste? Not necessarily. I came up with a good analytic insight for a paper. Is that a waste? I read on the beach. Surely that's not a waste! I still feel I've wasted much of the day. Obsessive.

My life it seems is a waster. I've done so much and yet I haven't done anything at all. I think You know what I mean. Only problem is that I don't know!

In my dreams last night I was reassigned—and created yet another parish and neighborhood, this one in the north suburbs on the lake, an Evanstonlike place. The shock of my transfer from CK returns again. It was so very real. Even when I woke up, it seemed real.

Of course I can't be transferred. I'm retired. However, I think it is keyed off my feelings during the day that I was not part of the archdiocese, which I have never been. And fortunate for me that I am not. You were wise and good in that.

Yet, I care so much about it. Maybe I do my work for Chicago better on the outside.

I love You.

July 24, 2001; 9:20 a.m.; Grand Beach
My Love,

Gosh, do I have a long memory. When I was calling a TV repair person, who is a good and reliable man, I had flashes of rude treatment from a long time ago, a record store salesman and a cop. I was angry all over again—not sustained anger, not rage, but I felt once again all the emotions that I felt so long ago.

I got over it at once. What made me angry was that they treated me with contempt. I don't like to be treated that way. Patently. Yet, it goes with being human that you are treated that way sometimes.

It's one of my weakness to flare up like that, though I usually keep it under control. Yet, with this paper in September to Catholic development directors, I am spoiling for a fight because I expect my work to be dismissed contemptuously.

I'll cool off before I go down to Orlando.

Anyway, control of rage will be a problem for me as long as I live. At least I have never replied to any e-mail idiots, which shows some wisdom.

I love You.

July 25, 2001; 8:30 a.m.; Grand Beach
My Love,

July is coming to an end. The heat wave is broken. It's gloomy and raining, all the better for my melancholy mood. However, I have a plan for the new novel which is nice.

Flashes of past memories continue, most of them of unpleasant interludes. Reviewing my life? A few flashes of pleasant interludes. Maybe there haven't been all that many. Oh, that's nonsense! There have been tons of them. Each day in the e-mail . . . Yet, the others remain. All the hurts and pains. Silly.

However, that's the way my memory works.

Too much time up here alone maybe.

Anyway, I love You.

July 30, 2001; 8:55 a.m.; Grand Beach

My Love,

July is winding down. So quickly does it pass. So quickly does time pass. So quickly does life pass. Nonetheless, I must be thankful for life and time and summer.

In a Bulgarian poem that Richard Wilbur has translated, the poet, a certain Valery hears kids in the street calling for one of their friends who is also named Valery. He recalls to mind when he was a kid and his friends called for him. He's tempted to open the window and cry out, "I can't come out today."

Comic, melancholy, insightful.

I watch the kids on the beach, six and under, playing exuberantly, trying as I say, to empty the lake into a hole in the beach. I identify with them. Yet, I also feel sorry for them, the little girls especially. They will have so many troubles in life. Their joy will be crushed, perhaps destroyed.

Why do You let that happen?

Silly question.

Just like the question, "Why must we die? Why must I die?"

Why must July come to an end?

Anyway, I am grateful for that . . . and for everything else.

I love You.

July 31, 2001; 7:30 a.m.; Grand Beach

My Love,

Yesterday on the beach, with the fog and the heat, this small girl child (not yet three) took offense at the sea birds (where do they nest, by the way?) and began to chase them, squawking at them in their own language. With considerable disdain, the birds lifted off the beach and then returned perhaps twenty yards away. They have learned enough to know that they don't have to fear the humans around here, especially the human kids. When the young girl returned to chase them again, they didn't even bother to run away. So she shouted more loudly. They departed once again, far enough away this time so that she was not offended.

Your creatures play such fun games.

And I sit and watch them and enjoy them and mourn for the child who will have to grow up and lose her carefree delight—as we all must.

For me, now, it is so hard to generate energy.

I love You.

August 2, 2001; 7:55 a.m.; Grand Beach

My Love,

In a poem by Linda Pastan ("The Coming on of Night") I read about a time when ambition, like a faulty pilot light, sputters and goes out, when we are left with the peace of evensong, when we sense night coming on even though yesterday it was only afternoon. It is almost time, she suggests, to feel our way out of the world.

Not quite D. Thomas railing against the failing of the light, is it?

One should go quietly and gratefully.

Not my time yet, I think. Yet, it comes closer.

Does ambition flutter and sputter? Sometimes. I am less interested in traveling everywhere to talk, as You well know. Yet, I still like to write, love it indeed.

So we work while we still have time, knowing that time is eventually going to run out—and we cling to your love.

And maybe enjoy a little the peace of evensong.

I love You.

August 7, 2001; 9:00 a.m.; Grand Beach

My Love,

I ponder the dragonflies, who dance above the pool in their elegant, graceful, erotic dance, while I swim. On the one hand, I exclaim what a brilliant show the Lord has made! On the other hand, I think that they live only a short time (they don't eat, as You know, because there is enough protein in them to keep them alive until they mate), and it all seems kind of pointless. Jesus would have us believe that not a dragonfly dies that You don't know about.

I believe that. I believe that the flight of the dragonflies reflects your beauty and your love. It would be a lot easier if You weren't so ineffable. But then You wouldn't be You, would You?

Am I little more than a dragonfly?

The answer to that is both yes and no, I believe.

But You do love me, that I know, though I often don't live that way.

I love You.

August 8, 2001; 8:50 a.m.; Grand Beach

My Love,

It continues to be very hot and humid. It's like a massive wall of heat and moisture hits me as soon as I go out the door. Big toxic spill on the expressway, shutting down much of the city. Poor firepersons are out there in their full regalia trying to clean it up. Terrible!

In Richard Wilbur's poem this morning he pictures You out there somewhere in space enjoying the show (not his words!). For all I know, it is much more glorious than Lake Michigan or the fireflies or the dragonflies. I'm sure it is. How much there is in the universe for You to delight in.

I should delight more in what is beautiful and reflective of You in my own tiny world.

I thank You for all the beauty with which You have surrounded me.

I wonder, do You take special delight in our little world? Or are You totally neutral on all these beauties?

I love You.

August 10, 2001; 9:45 p.m.; Grand Beach

My Love,

I have been working the last couple of days on the manuscript for Sheed & Ward's publication of my journals of the last couple of years. I must reflect on these in the days ahead. It's the first time I've ever read through one of them. I hold nothing back, which may make me look like a crybaby and a neurotic. I guess I don't care or I wouldn't let them publish it. To hell with those who will think less of me. Trouble is, I like myself less because I am a crybaby and a neurotic.

But one who loves You.

August 11, 2001; 11:14 a.m.; Grand Beach

My Love,

One lesson that emerged from reading my journal for the last three years is how many colds I've had. It's been five months since the last one, and I've almost forgotten what it's like. I now remember how sick I was last winter—and that wasn't in the journal. Most of it seems to come from riding airplanes, which in itself wears me out (and about which I complain repeatedly in the journal).

Yet, I am going on this wild-goose chase to Orlando next month and this equally silly trip to Los Angeles for the ASA next weekend. How dumb can I be. It is simply necessary to curtail plane flights. I will definitely leave Tucson only once this winter, just as I have left Grand Beach only once this summer.

Last night I saw *The Road Home,* a Zang Yimou film about young love in rural China. It was a sentimental idyll but still authentic. Our loves grow old and die as we do, too, but something remains, indeed a lot more than Zang seems to realize.

Anyway, I believe that no love ever dies in your mind. And neither does any lover.

I love You.

August 13, 2001; 9:16 p.m.; Grand Beach

My Love,

I skied this morning and am very proud of myself and very tired, even after a nap this afternoon. Maybe I stayed up too long!

A man's body washed up on the beach tonight. He had been missing for a couple of weeks. Why don't people realize how dangerous this lake is! Take care of him. I know You love him. Bring him home safe and sound to yourself, like the mother in Paddy Daly's poem.

I'm still not over the shock of reading my journal all the way through. I notice again how easily discouraged I am when I'm tired (as I am now!), and then I become angry. So I must not let myself be tired, I guess.

So I'm going to bed now.

I love You.

August 14, 2001; 4:19 p.m.; Grand Beach

My Love,

I still reflect on the body that washed up on the shore last night. I don't even know his name. What did he think when he found himself in the water? What did he think when he knew he was drowning? Then when he gave up completely and lost consciousness, what were his last feelings?

And then when he encountered You and new that goodness and love had saved him?

What is eternity like?

Eye has not seen . . . ?

Well, yes.

Take care of him, I beg You. Take care of all of us.

I love You.

August 15, 2001; 7:45 a.m.; Grand Beach

My Love,

I think I'm not as good at hospitality as I used to be. I still entertain guests and I still am courteous and friendly and make people feel welcome. But I like the work less and less. I feel that time is being wrenched away from me. I'm not as careful in what I do. Thus, last night I ruined the rice.

The secret perhaps is to take the guests out for supper. Easier on all concerned.

I'm not very good as a housewife. Perhaps what's surprising is that I've been able to play the role so long.

Getting old, I fear.

But that goes with the territory, doesn't it?

I love You.

August 16, 2001; 10:09 a.m.; Grand Beach

My Love,

Drab day. Kind of nice, however. There's a part of me that likes to wake up in the morning and hear rain on the roof, even if I know that it means the day will be cold and dreary. In principle, it should be a day when I'm under less pressure, free from a few demands. That's an illusion, of course.

You have wisely arranged matters so that there is a rhythm in nature and in human relationships: good times and not so good, rainy days and sunny days. Days like today, when water drips everywhere, and days when the air is crisp and clean and try. Night and day.

How much I should try to enjoy everything in your creation.

The peace process in Ireland is falling apart. Please help save it.

I love You.

August 23, 2001; 4:55 p.m.; Grand Beach
My Love,

A solid week since my last reflection and prayer. I'm sorry.

My trip out to the ASA convention in Anaheim was a nightmare. It took a good thirty-six hours to recover—which is no excuse for putting off these reflections. I flamed out as the day went on, but I guess I made a good impression, represented the priesthood and the Church as I had hoped I would. Not that what I can do will cancel out things like the five million dollar pedophile settlement in LA the same day!

August has not had much good weather. Summer winds down. I'm sorry for the lost opportunities.

I find myself thinking that my contribution, for whatever it's worth, is almost over. Maybe it is, but I don't think I'm slowing down, save for tiring more easily.

But that's a silly issue, isn't it? I'll do my best while I have time, no matter how little or how much time.

I've been rereading—or perhaps reading for the first time—my Chucky books. Maybe a half million words that recreate the years of this century. They're pretty good, much of the time. I wonder if anyone will look at them in years to come for what they are: a saga of the century.

That's not my problem though. My challenge is to make the next volume the best yet. Help me to do that.

I love You.

August 24, 2001; 11:14 a.m.; Grand Beach
My Love,

As I continue to read through the Chuck saga, I am impressed by how exciting the era was through which I have lived. Most people today don't know the early years of this century, about which I write. Hence they don't value enough the blessings (in this country and for whites) of the later years. For this perspective, I am grateful.

I also wonder whether people will read the saga in years to come. I doubt it. I feel like it's one more failure, though an ingenious and at times brilliant one. Anyway, after I'm gone, what does it matter what people say or think?

That's pretty melancholy, isn't it, but it's the end of summer!

I love You.

August 25, 2001; 1:24 p.m.; Grand Beach

My Love,

Terrible rain. Melancholy day. Everything gray. End-of-the-world kind of day! Second Saturday with Mass inside. New record.

I learned the story of the man whose body washed ashore last week and for whom the coast guard was hunting the week before. He had been out on the lake in a small boat of some sort with his twin nine-year-old daughters. One of the kids went over the side. Naturally he went after her. He managed to get her back in the boat, but hit his head on the ledge of the boat and drowned.

Okay, he was out too far and he didn't have a life jacket on. But the story makes me weep. I'm sure You are sad, too. I don't know how You're sad, and I don't know why You'd be sad about such silly creatures as we are. But I know You (equivalently somehow) weep for the man and his wife and their kids, and that You will try to wipe away all their tears—just as You weep for everyone that dies.

At least You do if You're the kind of God You claim to be—and I know You are.

You are concerned about me too, more than I could possibly be concerned about myself. Take care of me, I beg You, and bring me home to yourself when it is my time.

I love You.

August 26, 2001; 10:51 p.m.; Grand Beach

My Love,

Late at night. No reason for letting it go so long. Well, lots of reasons, which You know, so I won't try to explain them to You.

I am very sad at the death of my friend Dick Murphy, a classy human being if there ever was one. Grant him peace and happiness as one of your beloved children. Also bring healing to his family and his friends, especially to Rita. Help me to do justice to him in the funeral homily on Tuesday.

Watched *Msgr. Renard* on TV tonight. Inspector Morse as priest. Brilliant performance. Would I have had such courage under similar circumstances? Probably not. Thank You for not putting me to the test. Than You for sustaining me in my own tests.

I love You.

August 28, 2001; 8:53 p.m.; Grand Beach

My Love,

Terribly tired. A lot of driving to wake and funeral and cemetery in the last two days. Very moving experience, however. Irish—faith as strong as ever. I almost wept a couple of times.

I love You.

August 31, 2001; 10:13 a.m.; Grand Beach

My Love,

Another huge and un-forecasted storm last night turned Chicago into a floodplain for the second time this summer. Perhaps we must return the city to its primal swamp . . . er, wetlands.

Nice weekend predicted. I don't believe that. It breaks the rules!

Labor Day weekend. End of summer, though the kids have all disappeared because school starts now routinely before Labor Day. Crime!

I kept my resolution about not working on fiction during the summer, but still didn't relax much. Maybe I can't. Maybe I never will. Maybe I should give it up. Maybe I should just thank You for the summer and for the goodness of life. And for vacations, however spoiled they might be by my own folly.

Bad dreams the night before last. Too much talk about the priesthood, the archdiocese, and the Church, all of which are in deep trouble and of their own making. It is good that I am on the margins. I can't understand how caring priests keep on taking it. I pray for them.

I love You.

September 1, 2001; 10:51 p.m.; Grand Beach

My Love,

The series of circumstances that led the *New York Times* to commission me to write an article for their series Writers on Writing, for a week from Monday, are astonishing. I never quite understand how You intervene in our world, and I am reluctant to ascribe anything as the result of direct intervention. But that this should all be decided late afternoon of the Friday of the Labor Day weekend, and in the way it was, suggests that You might have been involved in some fashion.

In any case, I am very grateful for this opportunity. It even gives me an opportunity to drag You into the *NYT* explicitly. We'll see if they want to exclude You.

Many good things can come from this article. I thank You very much. A good way to end the summer. Thank You.

I love You.

September 2, 2001; 11:23 a.m.; Grand Beach

My Love,

Last Sunday of summer. Much melancholy feeling. How many more summers? None of my business. My business is to enjoy each one of them as they come, and also to enjoy Chicago as a sacrament of your love when I return.

I continue to fiddle with the *NYT* piece to polish it and make it harder for them to refuse.

I love You.

September 3, 2001 (Labor Day); 11:15 a.m.; Grand Beach

My Love,

Well, I celebrated Labor Day this morning by waterskiing and thus proved that, despite my erratic performance this summer, I can still do it. For which, many thanks. As I have reported to You previously, it both exhilarates and exhausts me. Not like the old days when I could ski all around Pine Lake!

A lovely day—the best Labor Day weekend ever. I wish summer didn't end and denounce the custom of it ending today. Yet, though I will stretch summer another week, I am not sticking to my commitment to stay here till October 1. A couple of things I simply can't refuse.

Anyway, thanks for the glory of summer which, here at Grand Beach, spills out all over and hints strongly at your glory—which, even in faint and pale hint, dazzles.

I love You.

September 4, 2001; 9:12 a.m.; Grand Beach

My Love,

I begin work today on a new novel. I've kept my promise of not doing any serious work this summer, though I'm not sure that made much difference in my life. I dread starting the work and the demands it imposes, and I look forward eagerly to getting it started. Help me to do a good job, especially since I want to write about who and what You are.

I love You.

September 5, 2001; 9:36 p.m.; Grand Beach

My Love,

Long day. Tired. I didn't get down to the beach. Packing, doing laundry, getting ready to leave. All sad. But I am grateful to You for everything, absolutely everything.

I love You.

September 8, 2001; 10:03 a.m.; Grand Beach
My Love,

Melancholy—and not just because of leaving the lake.

I'm working on the novel about a man who is disillusioned about both church and government. Jimmy Carter is president, the pope doesn't get it, and the archdiocese is in trouble. Not much different from the way things are now, so the book depresses me. We all get old and become cynical and disillusioned. Better that we realize that there are some things we can't change, and we should embrace the good that we have and get on with life. Hard to do, hard to write about.

I love You.

September 9, 2001; 10:48 a.m.; Grand Beach
My Love,

Last day here. Rain and humidity and hot sun. Don't want to go home, as I have made clear to You before. I thought briefly of the weekend in October I've protected. I'd just come up here and relax and enjoy the scenery.

Sure!

My assumption that I would ever relax anywhere and not work is foolish. Even if I didn't work on a novel till this week and did no sociology at all, I still was rushing all the time. That's the nature of my life, at least as I have constructed it. My own fault.

It's so beautiful up here, so very beautiful. I know You're everywhere, though I don't pay much attention. I'm sorry.

I'm a failure as a human being. What would I say to someone else who was surrounded by so much beauty and paid no attention to it? I'd call him an *eejit.*

Sorry, so sorry, for being an eejit.

Now I must rush to finish my packing.

I love You.

September 11, 2001; 4:32 p.m.; Chicago
My Love,

I'm still trying to cope with the dimensions of the terrible tragedy in New York. Thousands, perhaps tens of thousands of people, may have died in the terrorist attack on the World Trade Center. Since I believe that You grieve when even one of us dies, I'm sure that You're grieving now. It's an act of war. I'm sure that there will be reprisals, which I guess are an act of self-defense. I don't know what else to think. I have turned off the TV for a while. I grieve with and pray for everyone involved. Heal them, save them, grant them peace, I beg You.

I love You.

September 12, 2001; 7:09 p.m.; Chicago

My Love,

I've managed to stay away from television most of the day. Terribly depressing situation. I turned in a new column in which I said the obvious Catholic priest thing. Revenge belongs to You, not to us. The cries of so many Americans, from the president on down, for revenge are scary. Well, it made me feel good to make the point. He has not spoken out against the abuse of Arab or Muslim Americans either.

I hope church leaders around the country are speaking out against it.

I should have gone to Mass yesterday; I was too tired.

Pretty tired now, too.

Please take care of the injured and the dying and the bereaved.

I love You.

September 13, 2001; 9:34 a.m.; Chicago

My Love,

I'm getting a lot of e-mail from friends overseas offering sympathy. Impressive. Also some idiot e-mail from people who feel good when they express their grief and/or rage to others.

The rage is bad, especially when the political leaders of the country encourage it.

I have written my column on the subject. I will preach on it Sunday. I am numbed by the horror of it all and angry less at the fanatics who did it than I am at the government officials, like the secretary of transportation, who use it as an occasion to showcase themselves.

I try not to watch television.

I pray for all the dead, including the killers, for whom not many people are praying.

I love You.

September 14, 2001; 4:42 p.m.; Chicago

My Love,

I intended to do the minutes of silence with the rest of the country, but I didn't get to it until 4:00. Incredibly busy days since I came back last Monday. Then the strain, the anger, the trauma of what happened in New York and D.C., and my impatience with the response—both from our leaders and from many ordinary Americans, especially the idiots who pick on Arabs and Muslims.

So much pain for so many people, their bodies and their lives torn apart. People keep asking the question, "Where was God?" I wonder where they think You are when a single premature baby dies—weeping for your children. I'll do my column next week on that.

I am reading a book of poems written about a stack of pictures the poet found from past years. Incredibly good. Appropriate for our reunion on Sunday, though the idiots who are running it have crumbed it up badly.

My temper is hair-trigger. I'm angry at everything, and there is much to be angry about. Yet, I have no real reason to complain. I should be grateful for the gift of life, even if it is a costly gift.

I love You.

September 16, 2001; 9:54 p.m.; Chicago

My Love,

The reunion today was a great grace, though it was not well organized. My homily, which focused on the immorality of revenge, was very well received, though it ran against the temper of the country. A number of people said they had changed their minds because of it.

Also, the reaction to my column that challenged the cries for war and revenge was very favorable—eight or nine to one. The haters were really angry, more angry than usual.

I am convinced that many Americans are rethinking their reactions. Apparently, people went to church who haven't been there for a long time. Silver lining, I suppose. The really good thing is that now we are concerned about security and intelligence, before someone comes along with an atomic bomb.

Thank You for helping me to speak in your name and to tell the people that You love our enemies, too, and that You expect us to pray for them. Perhaps we progress.

I love You.

September 17, 2001; 9:15 a.m.; Chicago

My Love,

It struck me again yesterday with my classmates that we are old. Some of us look older than others, but we're all old. 'Course, we're all in our seventies, which is old by definition. I don't feel old most of the time. When I get a good night's sleep, as I have for the last three nights, I don't feel old at all, especially if there is a swim in the day. I did water-ski this summer. Yet, in truth, I am old.

All the young women I had crushes on are old too, some of them still beautiful, some of them happy, some of them not. Some have had very hard lives, which doesn't seem fair; they were once so bright and happy and hopeful.

I must leave them to You and to my faith, that You wipe away all the tears. Take good care of them for me, I beg You.

I love You.

September 18, 2001; 9:24 a.m.; Chicago

My Love,

The goofiness in D.C. continues as everyone talks of war. It's an abuse of language, a bad metaphor, an attempt to whip up a spirit of hatred and revenge in a country where there is too much of that spirit already.

American Airlines cancelled our trip to Zurich. Now we'll have to get there via Stockholm! People tell me that it's dangerous to go. I don't see that. Vienna and Zurich may be less dangerous than Chicago. Anyway, you can't live looking over your shoulder. I continue to rush. Austria might be a relief.

I love You.

September 19, 2001; 8:48 a.m.; Chicago

My Love,

Yesterday on TV a young black woman spoke at a memorial service for her father. It was a heartbreaking interlude, filled with that deep religious faith that is part of African-American culture.

So many broken hearts. Dear God, please heal them as quickly as You can.

The president called on the world, including the Islamic nations, to join his "crusade" against terrorism. That's like asking Jews to join a pogrom. Too many people are saying that we must rally round "our" president in this time of crisis. Even when he scares the rest of the world with his cowboy talk?

Bad times.

I'm clearly in dissent again and have no regrets about it either.

Give me the faith to continue.

I love You.

September 21, 2001; 2:57 p.m.; Chicago

My Love,

The country is in a mess. The stock market is falling, people are frightened, the airline industry is in a mess, we are on hold.

I find myself impatient with this. We (that is to say the airline industry) brought it on ourselves by being negligent on security and intelligence. For all the annoyance at the airport, they didn't do a good job. The whole country is paying the price of corporate greed. The government should indict them and nationalize the industry. They won't, of course, not while the GOP is running the country.

The president claimed last night that You were on our side because we are good and the other guys are evil. That's blasphemy and idolatry. He wasn't speaking for me. I want to make that clear.

Please take care of all those who are suffering and lonely, of our military rank and file who are risking their lives, of the ordinary people who are so frightened.

I believe that we will pull ourselves out of our national funk. However, the media are certainly prolonging it by the idiocy of their commentaries.

Take care of me on the trip I'm taking on Monday.

I love You.

September 22, 2001; 9:49 a.m.; Chicago

My Love,

My second column about the "war" is out. The good and the hostile reactions even out so far. The hostile reactions, however, worry me because they show how sick some elements are in our society. The column, as You know, was about revenge, about how You claim it as your own. The typical hostile reaction says, "Bomb the shit out of them." Quite literally. The person who sent it probably thinks he is a good Christian, too!

I grow uneasy about our trip to Vienna. In two weeks Bush may start bombing, and that makes our return more complicated. Well, I won't be a coward and turn back.

The country is in a mix of panic and funk. Not good. We'll survive it, but it's a bad, bad time.

Help us, I beg You.

I love You.

September 22, 2001; 8:32 p.m.; Chicago

My Love,

Turns out I've already done today's reflection. I think this is the first time I've done two in one day. Well, tomorrow will be busy.

I'm in a hurry to get away from all the anger and vengeance that television has whipped up in this country. Maybe some of it will be over by the time I get back.

Yet, there were lots of people down on Michigan Avenue today, getting on with life. Your Son said let the dead bury their dead, which is a hard saying but psychologically as well as religiously true. Life must go on, but the rage doesn't help.

I'm in a grim mood tonight. Nice wedding: beautiful, rich, charming, and utterly secular people. I told my strawberry story, which they all liked, of course. It's not their fault they don't know You. It's our fault. Their youth and beauty made me feel old and weary. *Weltsmerz.* What a nice world.

It doesn't last long, however. Like I say, life goes on.

I love You.

October 7, 2001; 2:35 p.m.; Chicago

My Love,

Home from a great trip. Exhausted, of course, and the usual cold. Still, thank you very much for the opportunities of the past ten days. I am truly very grateful, even though I'm going to bed now.

I love You.

October 8, 2001; 8:29 a.m.; Chicago

My Love,

There is so much fear in this country. Bin Laden's statement on TV yesterday, that America was frightened, north to south, east to west, was perfectly valid. One person I know fears that the terrorists are sitting, at this moment, in the lobby of the Four Seasons. From not paying any attention to them, we are now in constant anxiety about them. It is 100 percent certain that there will be counter-terror to our idiotic little bombing campaign, we are told. If our leaders are that certain, why don't they find the people that are going to do it and stop them?

Our guide in Hungary asked if we were afraid. We both said we were not. Life is precarious and fragile. We can be run over by cars, gunned down by some mad person, infected by the West Nile virus, obliterated by a return of the Spanish influenza, killed in an airplane crash attributable to pilot error. Far more people are killed by guns in this country than died in the World Trade Center.

We must resign ourselves to dying, one way or another. Most death is messy, some of it is horrible. Yet, it will happen. We should be more aware of death and less frightened by it as a result of what happened on September 11.

The country is not ready for that, however. I'm just a little ashamed by the behavior of so many Americans, though the media have whipped up the fear and are to be blamed for the worst of it.

Anyway, I accept my death, whenever and however it comes. I have had a good and an exciting life. I have no cause for complaints.

I love You.

October 10, 2001; 8:07 a.m.; Chicago

My Love,

I'm still suffering from jet lag and from a cold. Not in very good humor!

Long interview with John Callaway yesterday for the *Chicago Stories* program. It went very well, despite my cold. A chance to review much of my life with a man who is sympathetic and had done me the courtesy of actually reading my book. Some reason to be hopeful this morning!

Do I need encouragement that much?

I love You.

October 11, 2001; 7:31 a.m.; Chicago

My Love,

Still limping along with this terrible cold. And trying to work and sort out my schedule and straighten out my office. Please hang in there with me.

I love You.

October 12, 2001; 8:09 a.m.; Chicago

My Love,

My cold seems to be waning. I sure hope so.

We saw *Hearts in Atlantis*, the wonderful, nostalgic film based on one of Stephen King's novels. Its theme of the power of young love reminded me of my first love, which ended when we moved away in 1938. Yet, we were in the same parish and only four blocks away.

In the film the boy moves away and doesn't write. The girl doesn't write either. Young love, for all its intensity, doesn't have much depth—or so it seems. Yet, I have never forgotten her and never will. Is she still alive? I wonder. Did she feel then that I had abandoned her? Doubtless I did, perhaps, because I felt that as someone who wanted to be a priest, I had no time for girlfriends. Maybe that was right. What did I know then? What do I know now?

Anyway, in your grace, we will meet again, and everything will be young again.

I ask You to protect her wherever she may be.

I love You.

October 13, 2001; 7:58 a.m.; Chicago

My Love,

The panic in the country is getting to me. The current anthrax scare is crazy, yet the government suggests that, well, maybe it is Osama. Muslim clerics and people around the world demonstrate against us, which puts the local Muslims on the spot. Perhaps we have excused them too easily. Self-serving arguments that Israel has nothing to do with the terrorism are silly. So much idiocy on the media. The country has been whipped into a frenzy of fear. The Sears Tower is suppose to disappear tomorrow. I kind of doubt all of this, but there seems to be no strong sense of reality in charge. Both the president and the vice president seem to have gone flaky. And they're putting concrete barriers around the building!

Maybe my persistent cold has left me jaded.

I love You.

October 14, 2001; 9:17 a.m.; Chicago

My Love,

Still sick. Two good weeks in Europe and now two bad weeks with a cold. Another week to go.

I have a baptism this afternoon out in Elmhurst. I have to go because the family would be upset if I bugged out. On the other hand, I don't want to infect the poor kid. I'm not sure I'm up to the drive. Everything is going wrong.

I love You.

October 17, 2001; 8:10 a.m.; Chicago

My Love,

Sunny day, but cold. Can't You keep winter away a little longer? Please! I understand perfectly well that You don't directly intervene in such matters, but I have to complain to someone!

The cold lingers. I went swimming last night and the pool seemed terribly cold. It was a relief to be able to swim again, however.

Only two days into the week and it's been a terrible week. However, the problems have resolved themselves, I guess.

It's so very hard to work on a novel with a cold. Yet, I have to do it. Why do I have to do it? Because I do—that's why. If I could work at my regular schedule of two thousand words a day, it would be fine. But other things in life won't let me do that.

I'm in a complaining mood this morning. Maybe that means I'm getting better.

I love You.

October 18, 2001; 7:13 p.m.; Chicago

My Love,

I am watching my life winding down and frittering away. As I grow older, more tired, and more susceptible to colds, I continue to work at the same frantic pace. This current novel is an obsession. I work on it every day, blindly pushing ahead and hoping that it all works, though I have no idea of whether it does. The other things in life crowd in around the fringes. I don't have much more time, even if I live ten years longer, though I think I live and work like I believe I'm immortal.

I don't think I'd terribly object to the end of my life, though I am afraid of the fuss and bother of dying.

Strange thing to say.

Monday night WTTW will celebrate me as a Chicago story. I will be brisk and insightful and funny with John Callaway as though I am not worn and weary and overwhelmed.

Fraud? Maybe. I don't know. I'm so tired.

That's the cold speaking, at least in part.

In a dream last night, was transferred again to a new parish. I said to the pastor, "I'm happy to move, CK was getting dull." I don't know what these dreams mean. I've had them so long. As usual, I had odd quarters of which I was trying to make the best, locking the windows against a summer wind—while outside, a fierce autumn wind was beating against the window.

Down to Grand Beach tomorrow for four nights. Time perhaps to recoup. Help me.

Tired, discouraged, ready to give up.

Still, I love You.

October 24, 2001; 9:29 a.m.; Chicago

My Love,

The TV program on channel 11 went well enough, though they cut too much of the interview about my novels, which was a shame.

The program also made me realize how old I am, both because I looked older than I thought I did and because so many of the events we talked about were so long ago. So, while the program was well done, it made me feel sad.

I also read a book on Monday by a distinguished scholar who is seventy. It was a good book, but there were no references after the early 1980s, and the chapters were stretched together in an awkward form. I know the field a little bit, and he left out a lot of important material. I suspect that it was a book written twenty years ago and rejected repeatedly, which it should not have been. Finally he found a generous publisher. I felt sorry for him and realized that, with age, one slows down.

Anyway, it was a good weekend at GB. I'll try to schedule another.

I love You.

October 25, 2001; 8:49 a.m.; Chicago

My Love,

At long—two and a half weeks—last, the cold seems to be over. Not a very pleasant interlude.

My R.A. told me yesterday that she and some of her friends had been to several memorial services in NYC for college classmates. She also told of a man I know who took his daughter and a bunch of her friends to dinner before the daughter went to the London office of her New York firm. All the friends are now dead.

These stories bring home the terrible pain of the terrorist murders in NY. Since You suffer when your children suffer, You must be suffering terribly. I'm afraid I've been so angered by the babbling of talking heads on TV that I have not realized the horror of the event. So many lives, young lives in these cases, have been broken. Grant everyone light and peace and healing.

Help me in my current discouragement.

I love You.

October 27, 2001; 9:42 a.m.; Chicago

My Love,

It's been three weeks now and traces of the cold persist. It drags me out as I try to work and finish the novel and make two more trips around the country before Christmas. Sorry to complain. It's better than having anthrax panic, which still sweeps the country.

Saw *Othello* last night. Terrible set, ridiculous costumes, stupid protagonist, great music. How dumb men can be.

My life slips away and I fiddle with little things. And today the time changes, which means it will grow darker even earlier. Ugh.

Still I praise You for the season.

I love You.

October 28, 2001; 9:28 a.m.; Chicago

My Love,

Bears game this afternoon. Nice day. Promising team for a change. Don't want to go. I'd rather stay here and work on finishing the novel. The latter is driving me crazy. Very worried that it doesn't work. Well, all I can do is try.

Very depressed by morning papers. American media utterly wrong on Ireland—still. Blame the IRA and the Catholics. More despair about government's handling of foolish war and terrorists and anthrax.

Sunday papers always depress me, now especially.

Country is in disgraceful panic.

I love You.

October 29, 2001; 8:41 a.m.; Chicago

My Love,

I'm still struggling with the novel and with my cold and with my unhappiness at the way this country is responding to terrorism—self-pity and panic. My spiritual life, I fear, is close to dead. I have to get the novel off my back, even though I am not satisfied with it. The first thing is to get it done. Then I can revise at leisure, more or less.

I'm going to NY this weekend. I don't want to, not because of the danger, but because it means the waste of another six days.

Terrible attitude. I'm sorry.

I love You.

October 30, 2001; 1:16 p.m.; Chicago

My Love,

I visited Brian Shannon at the hospital today. The transplant was a success, but he has somehow contracted pneumonia. Doesn't seem to have much of a chance. He's been a gallant survivor through the years. Please take care of him for us and, if it be your will, give him back to us for more years.

Hospitals are depressing places. However, someone stopped me to give me a flu shot, which was a good work. Thank You for hospitals and flu shots and all the other things that have given us more life and better health. Now, if You could arrange to get rid of this cold I'd be very happy.

I'm so tired of the novel. I'm sure it's not working.

Anyway, I love You.

November 7, 2001; 8:48 a.m.; Chicago

My Love,

Back home after a good time in NYC and a transcendent performance of *La Traviata* at the met—Verdi's most Catholic opera.

Received the first copies of the new edition of these reflections. Didn't like. I'm a whiner and a complainer. Sorry.

Feeling better now, finally. After a month-long cold. I'll finish the novel tomorrow, I hope. Then I'll get my life back on track. It's been a chaotic autumn.

I'm sorry about that too. But grateful for all the good things in the last two months.

Christmas looms ahead with all the rush and the aggravations. Each year I resolve that I will not let them get to me—and each year they do. This year I'll try to do better. But I'll need a lot of your help.

I love You.

November 8, 2001; 8:57 a.m.; Grand Beach

My Love,

I visited my friend Brian again yesterday. He had slipped a little since the day before. What a terribly difficult road he has had to walk. I'm not sure that I could survive anything that painful. Please help him to get better.

I will finish the novel today. It is the most difficult yet, both because of the subject matter of midlife, and because of the circumstances under which I had to write it.

Poetry had only one good poem this month. It is a translation of the Anglo-Saxon poem "Deor." The poet says his name is known and that he sang until another singer took his place. Then he concludes (every stanza) with the line: "All that has passed and so will this."

That summarizes human life, does it not?

My songs will pass and be forgotten. What counts, however, is that I sang them.

I love You.